Finding Our Voice

Finding Our Voice

Searching for Renewal in the Mainline Church

Neil M. Glover

SAINT ANDREW PRESS
Edinburgh

First published in 2024 by

SAINT ANDREW PRESS
121 George Street
Edinburgh EH2 4YN

Copyright © Neil M. Glover 2024

ISBN 978-1-80083-051-6

Scripture quotations are from New Revised Standard Version
Bible: Anglicized Edition, copyright © 1989, 1995 National
Council of the Churches of Christ in the United States of
America. Used by permission. All rights reserved worldwide.
Other versions are indicated in the text.

British Library Cataloguing in Publication Data

A catalogue record for this book is available from the British Library.

It is the publisher's policy to only use papers that are natural and
recyclable and that have been manufactured from timber grown
in renewable, properly managed forests. All of the manufacturing
processes of the papers are expected to conform to the environmental
regulations of the country of origin.

Typeset by Regent Typesetting
Printed and bound in the United Kingdom by
CPI Group (UK) Ltd

Contents

To my mum and dad,
Robert and Elizabeth Glover,
and in memory of
Graham Maule
who helped me find what needed to be found

Introduction

The origins of this book lie in many moments: a German professor going for a walk with his dogs; the rediscovery of a much-loved Scottish band; an Irish priest interrupting an all-age service; long minutes kneeling on a hard concrete floor in India; witnessing a friend almost die on a French glacier. Thoughts have been formed through numerous coffees, arguments, surprising encounters, disappointing initiatives, online conversations and even in meetings. It is with one such meeting that we begin: at the offices of an Edinburgh marketing agency in early 2015.

Throughout the early 2010s, the committee which had responsibility for the recruitment and training of Church of Scotland ministers, of which I was a part, was becoming increasingly concerned at a forthcoming drop in ministerial numbers. Very few candidates were coming forward for training and huge numbers of existing ministers were about to retire.

I had thought a lot about that group of retirees, one of whom was my own dad, and I had witnessed his ministry, alongside those of his colleagues, at close quarters for the previous thirty years. Having trained in packed theology faculties throughout the 1970s and 1980s, theirs was a generation possessed of remarkable gifts and energy, who had hoped to see the Church break away from the restrictions of the past and find its purpose within modern Scotland. The Church which would serve communities experiencing the traumatic loss of heavy industry and moving into the uncertain patterns of the service economy. The Church which would speak truth to power in a country which still listened to our General Assembly. The Church which would find contemporary language for an ancient gospel and fulfil one of its oldest aspirations, to be reformed and to keep reforming.

That retiring generation had achieved many things, but there was one thing which they had not managed to do. They had not managed to halt the precipitous decline of the Church of Scotland's membership, a decline which began in the 1950s and continues to this day. They had witnessed the arrivals of Gen X, Gen Y and Gen Z; the internet and then social media. They had prayed and marched for peace during wars and conflicts in Northern Ireland, Iraq and Afghanistan; and society had undergone huge cultural changes. Yet through all of this there had been one constant: the rate of decline of Scotland's national Church. Reports had been written and initiatives launched; pews had been replaced by flexible seating, hymnbooks by screens, organs by keyboards; congregations had been linked and united; there had been strategies and targets and plans but the loss had continued unabated.

The ever-growing shortage of ministers was but one symptom of this wider decline, a decline which we wanted to help reverse. In recruiting more ministers, we were hoping for a new generation of energised and radical leaders who might become the catalyst for wholesale transformation, but surely such a hope was utter hubris. In this, how could we possibly succeed when that earlier generation, with all their talents, had not?

Around the marketing agency's offices were posters from a recent campaign on behalf of the Scottish tourist industry. Dramatic shots of castles and glens were juxtaposed with images of modern Scotland: the tartan was stylish and the Scots wearing it were young and chic, with perfect teeth and perfect beards. We realised that to recruit new ministers, we needed to project an image of ourselves which was more aligned with this new emerging Scotland.

There was significant irony in the venue for our meeting: the marketing agency's offices had previously been a church. All around us were monuments to the building's former life: stained-glass windows; the pipes of a disused organ, the words 'God is love' emblazoned on the wall. Somehow this building was both a symbol of what we were wanting to become, re-energised and contemporary; and yet also a symbol of what we were seeking to avoid, because the congregation which used to worship here was no more.

With the aid of flip-pads and post-it notes we explained to the marketeers, as best we could, the job of a minister. They were aghast at the complexity of our committee-based training processes, but they were not unsympathetic. After all, the Church did a lot of good, and these ambitious creatives loved the challenge of a rebrand.

Towards the end of our session, the chairman of the company came down to join us. He had a certain presence. His glasses, his hair, his tailored waistcoat all said 'success'. The other marketeers might be good, but he was the guru. He was indeed pleased to be helping an institution as worthy as the Church of Scotland. Having listened to a summary of our discussion, he shared in the collective horror at our labyrinthine processes but blessed our ideas for recruitment and bestowed his approval. And then, as he got ready to leave, he recalled a memory which had just resurfaced in his mind ... 'Do you know,' he said, 'I don't go to a Church of Scotland, I don't go to church at all, but I used to. The school I went to was a boarding school. Every Sunday we would put on our best school uniform, our blazers and our kilts, and we would march out of the boarding house, down the main street, and into the church ...' He paused to let us picture the scene. And then he voiced a memory shared by millions of Scots: 'It was easily the most boring hour of my week.'

We all laughed because he had told a funny story ... and we all laughed because it was true.

I have many memories of that marketing campaign, 'Tomorrow's Calling' as it was later called. It painted a bold and inspiring vision of ministry in contemporary Scotland. We showed ministers with young people, in prisons, in schools, one was even pictured adjacent to a helicopter. Our first film was picked up by national media and I ended up on the sofa of a late-evening news programme discussing the campaign's significance. Modern Scotland was interested in our message.

The campaign also seemed to strike a chord with its most important audience – those who might become ministers. Over the next few years, the number of trainee ministers either held steady, or even rose – one exceptional year saw one of the largest cohorts in decades. And yet, the change was only temporary; and the wider, institutional change for which we had quietly hoped? That never came. As the memory of Tomorrow's Calling receded, so too did the number of new recruits.

Perhaps we need to return to the marketeers, hold another crisis meeting, and launch a new initiative. Perhaps, but I suspect this would only give a temporary boost. The number of new ministers is not our root problem. Neither is the complexity of our training process, nor even the culture of committees which created it. Our core problem lies deeper. I believe it lies within the memory of that marketing guru, in the memory of millions of Scots, shared across the western world, that going to church was 'the most boring hour of my week'.

Why did the Church's pews become the venue for so much boredom? Was it because people resented the fact that they were forced to attend? Was it because television and then social media decreased attention spans and traditional Church services became increasingly anachronistic in a postmodern society? These may all have been factors, but I do not believe they identify our core problem.

True boredom is not about the failure to be entertained, but is the symptom of a much deeper malaise: it is the sign of a fundamental disconnection, an estrangement between us in the Church and our communities, between us and ourselves and, yes, between us and God. Ultimately its roots are spiritual, they lie at the very deepest levels of our identity and our faith.

This book is about how we might understand and come to repair this deeper malaise: that in the last few decades, we in the Church of Scotland, alongside the wider family of mainline Protestant churches,[1] have lost much of our confidence, our vocation and, if we are honest, something of our faith. Renewal does not necessarily mean a recovery of our numbers, but it does mean recovering those three things: confidence, vocation and faith.

This is not a new quest but, as we shall explore, our attempts at renewal too often sit at the level of structural reconfiguration rather than spiritual renewal. We fail to understand the long, historic patterns which have led us to where we are. We fixate on what we lack rather than build on the gifts we already have. And too often we borrow from other realms without sufficiently reclaiming what it is to be a church and, in particular, what it is to be a mainline church.

Throughout this book we will engage with our own story and with more contemporary stories which might inspire. The hope is that these will give us clues to our own renewal: not by way of slavish imitation but rather that these stories might help us discover our own calling. God, it seems, never wants us to mimic someone else's salvation, but rather to work out our own (Phil. 2:12–13).

I am writing as a minister of almost twenty years who has benefited from the varied experiences of working in urban and rural parishes, national and regional committees (I currently chair a group which funds new worshipping communities). I have long associations with a group of evangelical Christian outdoor centres and an ecumenical worship group, and am co-presenter of a podcast, and have lived in Northern Ireland and India. I am married to Anna, a secondary school guidance teacher, and with her a parent to three teenage children.

Many of the ideas and stories in this book were born in the life of the Church of Scotland but they are paralleled across the whole of the mainline Church. In particular, my hope is to tell another story of the mainline Church; a story which is the opposite of that marketing guru's 'most boring hour of the week'; a story of being renewed, which may or may not mean the recovery of our numbers but will mean the finding of our voice.

For me, the finding of our voice has become epitomised in one particular story which is almost embarrassingly non-religious. In the early 2010s I was chaplain to a secondary school on the outer edge of Glasgow. The occasion was the school's end-of-term concert, which was a brilliant occasion: dedicated pupils, many of whom I knew, who gave a range of superb performances. Towards the end of the second half, however, three girls appeared at the side of the stage who looked very different. They weren't wearing full uniform, didn't play any instruments and, among the school's star performers, didn't look like they wholly fitted in. However, for one of the teachers it was clearly very important that these girls sang. When their turn came, she took extra care of them, calmed their nerves, and got them ready. The three girls walked up the steps on to the stage, stood very near the back and nervously waited for the backing track to begin. It was 'Let It Go' from *Frozen*. As the moment came for the girls to start singing, they looked at each other anxiously and gripped each other's hands; we in the audience perhaps anticipated a performance which might not reach the heights of the rest of the programme, but we were willing them on.

And then they sang. Oh what a sound. The power of it.

Though I had heard 'Let It Go' hundreds of times, this was different. These girls sang as if this was *their* song; somehow it felt like the music, with inexplicable power, was flowing through them. We in the audience were in awe, and not a few of us in tears.

Because these girls had worked at this, because they had found one another, because they had been encouraged, they sang in a way which made the song utterly true, utterly new and utterly alive. And in us who heard, something happened which we couldn't fully explain.

That is what it is to find our voice.

(Quotations are taken from the NRSV other than when indicated in the text: English Standard Version (ESV); *The Message* (MSG); and the author's own translations.)

PART I

Turn

I

Loss

Before speaking of renewal, we must speak of loss. This is a law of the spiritual life.

Whether it is David crying, 'How long. O Lord?' before he sings '[the Lord] has dealt bountifully with me' (Ps. 13), or Naomi demanding to be called 'bitter' before the unlikely events which bring a grandson into her arms (Ruth 1 and 4), the scriptures teach us that the path to authentic hope travels through the naming and lamenting of loss.

Our churches have experienced loss and we know this too well: the emptiness of a once-filled sanctuary or the pain of a building being closed; parents seeing their children, once they are adults, finding little connection with the Church in which they had been baptised; the veteran Sunday school teacher, unable to find a successor, who prepares lessons for two or one or perhaps no children; the minister exhausted by multiple parishes and wondering when they might retire; the ever-increasing pressures of governance being shouldered by a decreasing and overworked few.

One could say 'we shouldn't be worried about numbers', or 'faith isn't about buildings', or 'it doesn't matter where they go, as long as they have a faith', but the loss still matters. The accompanying sense of failure gnaws at us, and we blame ourselves, our leaders, our committees. We blame Sunday sports leagues, social media and, yes, even God. The graph overleaf shows the decline in my own context of Church of Scotland membership since 1901.

It is a graph of two halves. For the first half of the twentieth century, the numbers are relatively stable *and* with slight rises as a result of an increasing population and the Church's role in

3

providing a civic rallying point after the Second World War. The second half is of steep and near-constant numerical decline, a decline which is shared by almost all mainline churches. What are its causes? There are several possible reasons.

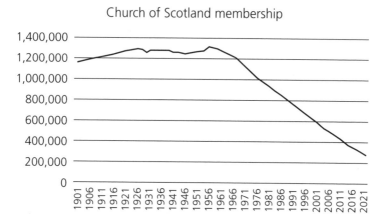

Church of Scotland membership

Lack of Resources

The first possible reason is that we do not have enough resources: not enough money, clergy, members or young people. If we can somehow increase the numbers of these, or perhaps even concentrate these into larger units, then some form of snowball-effect might trigger a more prolonged expansion. There are many objections to be made to this argument, but for now we should simply note the constant gradient of the Church of Scotland's decline. The well-resourced Church of the 1960s and 1970s (with its large Sunday Schools and Youth Fellowships) declined at exactly the same rate as the moderately resourced Church of the 1980s and 1990s, and at almost exactly the same rate as the considerably more fragile Church of the 2000s. During that time, we have continually merged smaller congregations into larger better-equipped congregations, and these have declined at exactly the same rate. Our decline has not been caused by lack of resources.

The Need for Change

Another oft-cited charge is that mainline churches have declined because of their love of the past and their inability to change. 'How many Presbyterians does it take to change a lightbulb? ... CHANGE??!!!' as the joke goes, with Anglican, Methodist and Congregationalist variations. However, in recent years, mainline denominations have not been short of proposals for radical change. In the Church of Scotland these have included those of the 'Committee of 40' in the 1970s, the 'Church Without Walls' report in the early 2000s, and the report of a particularly bold special commission in 2019. Every mainline denomination could cite similar proposals, proposals which have often led to costly, far-reaching and sometimes extremely painful change. And yet none of these changes, it would appear, has given birth to decline-reversing transformation.

Perhaps this is because we lack the courage to make the truly radical change which our reports very often propose, to say goodbye to our sacred cows. However, I have become convinced that there is no 'magic lever', the pulling of which (should we find it, should we possess enough courage to pull) will lead to the reversal of our decline. In 2015, Steve Salyards, a lover of all things Presbyterian, posted a graph on his GA junkie blog, which showed that since the early 2000s the Presbyterian Church of the USA (the PC(USA)) had declined at exactly the same rate as the Church of Scotland (uncannily so). This seemingly unremarkable graph has had a profound effect on my own understanding of denominational change. First, it showed that we in the Church of Scotland were not faring as uniquely badly as I had presumed. Second, I have been party to many discussions in which it was suggested that the Church of Scotland might be revived if we had sufficient courage and determination to drop our commitment to being a national Church, or to recruit sufficient ministers, or to train those ministers in church-specific seminaries (and insist they learn Greek!), or to permit only congregations with sufficient finance to call a minister. Every single one of these conditions exists in the PC(USA) and yet its rate of decline is exactly the same as the Church of Scotland's.

There is no change of the 'magic lever' variety which might enable our transformation. Mainline denominations in Canada, England, Wales, New Zealand, the Netherlands, Scotland and the United States[1] have almost exactly the same rates of decline (again, uncannily so) regardless of the levers they have pulled. For a number of years it looked like bishop-led mainline denominations, with their emphasis on person-centred leadership, were experiencing a slower rate of loss, but since the mid-2010s their rates of decline have also begun to match those of their committee-led counterparts.

These 'magic lever' changes all fit the description of 'technical change':[2] known solutions which are followed in response to a known problem. What of 'adaptive change' which is required when we live in a new environment, and goes deeper than technical change, addressing our culture, values and identity? Here we are certainly closer to the kind of change to which we are called, but even these approaches fail to deliver renewal[3] if they do not address the most fundamental aspect of our identity: our relationship with and understanding of God. We shall return to this theme shortly, but given the considerable changes undergone and embraced by mainline churches since the 1950s we should not identify a general resistance to change as the primary source of mainline decline.

A Changed Culture

The true cause of mainline decline becomes apparent when we discover that mainline denominations all started their decline within the same ten-year period, from about 1955–1965, and that this near identical and precipitous decline has been experienced in countries which have undergone the cultural phenomenon known as 'Secularisation'.[4]

The roots of Secularisation can be traced back to the late Middle Ages, but its influence is considerably more recent. In the 1950s and 1960s, without the pressure for civic unity which had been essential after the Second World War, and with rising household wealth, Secularisation began to take root in western societies, especially in those where Protestantism had been the dominant religious force.[5] Two of Secularisation's salient features are of critical importance in understanding its effect on the mainline Church:[6]

1 Secularisation is the rise of non-belief. Increasingly, people do not believe in gods, ghosts or spirits. Sometimes referred to as 'Disenchantment', this decline in religious belief has understandably brought a corresponding decline in overall church attendance.

2 Secularisation is the emergence of religious choice, including the choice not to believe. This emergence is closely related to the 'turn to the self', which entails us, as individuals, shaping our identity in response to our own inner values rather than our identity being conferred by external norms. This aspect of Secularisation has led to a diminishment of the Church's central social status, sometimes referred to as the end of Christendom, and has particularly affected those churches where cultural expectation or social respectability were some of the principal reasons for membership.[7]

In 2001, the sociologists Linda Woodhead and Paul Heelas conducted a famous experiment on the relationship between Church decline and Secularisation.[8] Using the northern English town of Kendal as their field of study, they categorised its congregations and spiritual groups according to two factors which were closely related to these two dimensions of Secularisation:

1 How different were the beliefs of the congregation or group from those of the surrounding culture? (Given that such a difference was derived from the group's belief in a God who is 'different' this, in effect, became a measure of their resistance to Disenchantment.)

2 How strongly did the congregation or group foster a person's individual growth (to what extent had it embraced the turn to the self)?

Following a rigorous analysis of congregational attendance, Woodhead and Heelas discovered that decline was significantly steeper in those congregations which

1 *had not* resisted Disenchantment, but
2 *had* resisted the turn to the self.

The first of these conclusions seems counterintuitive – surely going with the cultural flow on Disenchantment would enhance attendance? Why does resistance to a culture's Disenchantment cause one to flourish within it? The second conclusion seems more explicable: churches which resist the turn to the self will struggle within societies which have embraced it. We shall return to both these findings in future chapters but for now we should simply note that when turning to Woodhead and Heelas's Appendix, to discover exactly which churches had made this apparently disastrous double-response to Secularisation, one discovers that these were the churches of the mainline. Secularisation has affected all churches, but it has visited particularly steep declines upon the mainline Church. We will explore the reasons for this, and how the mainline Church might respond, throughout Part 1 of this book.

The End?

Before closing this chapter on loss, it is important, though also slightly terrifying, to face another feature of graphs on mainline membership: the possibility that the line may hit zero. If the pace of decline continues at its current rate then, for the Church of Scotland, this moment will occur in just over ten years.

The American Episcopalian Barbara Brown Taylor tells the story of visiting, in modern-day Turkey, the ruins of a twelfth-century cathedral which had been built by the ancient but now vanished Christian kingdom of Georgia. Walking around the cathedral's ruined walls, Taylor was overwhelmed by its vast size and the grandeur of what it had once been; yet side-chapels were now rubbish tips and children played football in the nave. 'It is one thing to talk about the post-Christian era,' she wrote, 'it is another to walk around inside it.'[9]

This could be our mainline future. Perhaps in ten years, or maybe, if the line starts to flatten a little, in thirty years, there will be no mainline churches left; our buildings abandoned or converted into houses, or warehouses or museums to the lost age of 'Mainline Christianity'.

For some, this loss will not be mourned: the mainline Church has abandoned the truth of the gospel and deserves no future. Others believe the mainline's chief purposes to have been fulfilled, with its great accomplishments of education and healthcare now safely passed into secular hands; the institution which birthed these things can now be granted a peaceful retirement. For yet others, institutional denominations belong to a passing age and the future belongs to near-autonomous congregations.

Perhaps, but I am unconvinced. I cannot agree with the American commentator who asserted: 'The death of the Mainline is the central historical fact of our time', and that its institutions are 'corpses, even if they don't quite realise they are dead'.[10]

By contrast, my experience of the mainline is that there is still much life: a stubborn, joyous, even surprising life. And with this life comes a resilient hope. Whether in congregations, or on the fringes or sometimes even at Synods and General Assemblies, there are still moments when we turn to our neighbour and say, 'Surely God is in this place.'

We mainliners may experience great change in our future structures, but I do not believe we will become extinct. The theologian Robert Jenson once wrote on the indelible link between possessing life now and the assurance of a future tomorrow: 'A live person or a community has a future, a dead person or community does not.'[11] In Jesus Christ, if you have life now, you have a future tomorrow. That is the deep truth of the resurrection.

'But what of that ancient Georgian ruin?' it may be asked. 'Its Church was once alive, but now is no more.' 'But has that Church been truly erased?' we might contend. Did no great-great-grand-children make it to some diaspora congregation in Greece, or

Cairo or Rome? Are its insights not still uttered in some still-remembered prayer? Are its saints not still with us, numbered among the Church ascended? In faith, might we believe that somehow, somewhere, the Church of twelfth-century Georgia is still alive?

I, for one, do not believe that the churches of the mainline will meet their demise in ten or thirty or even a hundred years. This conviction depends on a yet to be extinguished hope, that life now means life tomorrow. And for now, that is enough.

2

God

It is probably the most important encounter in the history of Israel.

An 80-year-old fugitive, minding sheep on the slopes of a desert mountain, turns to investigate a mysterious fire. He has spotted flames from a small bush, not unusual in this wilderness with its scorching heat and absence of water; but this fire is strange, the branches of the bush are not being consumed. Drawing closer, he hears a voice; and now the mystery deepens because somehow the voice knows his name:

'Moses! Moses! ... take off your shoes, you are standing on holy ground.'

At first this was only a perplexing phenomenon, it might even have been an angel, but now the voice reveals its true nature ... 'I am God.' But this is not God emerging from nothing, this is God emerging from an older story ('the God of your father, the God of Abraham, the God of Isaac and the God of Jacob') and a community's long and continuous yearning ('I have heard their cry').

God, it transpires, has a job for this octogenarian shepherd. He has heard the cries of his people, the children of Israel, enslaved in Egypt, and Moses is to lead them out.

For Moses, there are some concerns.

'Who am I, to go to Pharaoh?' he asks.

'I will be with you,' says God.

This does not remove all of Moses' anxiety ...

'So I am going to the children of Israel and will say to them, "The God of your fathers has sent me to you." When they say to me, "What is his name?" what shall I say to them?'

And God said to Moses, 'I am who I am.'

The name is both evocative and elusive. To say 'I am who I am' or 'I will be who I will be' (the Hebrew can mean either) is to say something definitive about God: that God fundamentally *is*, and that God will be further revealed in the seismic events to follow. But this name is also mysterious and unknowable. God can only be described by further reference to God, and any other vocabulary must at this moment be refused because even the best words might constrain the one who is beyond the limits of language.

We know the rest of the story: the plagues, the Passover, the parting of the Red Sea, the Commandments, the forty years of wandering, and eventually the Promised Land. Through all of this, Moses will continue to meet with God, his face radiant after each encounter. For renewal is always begun and sustained through encounter with the presence of God.

There are similar themes in the call of Jesus. His ministry begins with baptism and heaven being torn open, the Spirit descending and a voice proclaiming, 'You are my Son, the Beloved' (Mark 1:11). The nearness of God is then shared with all humanity as Jesus begins his ministry with the proclamation: 'the kingdom of God has come near, turn and believe the good news' (Mark 1:15, my own translation).

The word 'turn' requires some explanation because it has often been translated into the word 'repent', a word which has connotations of repeatedly saying sorry for our sins until a reluctant God tempers his disapproval. Rather, the word 'turn', or *metanoia* in the Greek, means to turn our whole being – our minds, our imaginations, our bodies, our intentions – away from what is false and diluted, and towards the God who is God. Just as 'turning' had been the crucial movement in the story of Moses, so also in Galilee the crowds are summoned by Jesus to turn towards the kingdom and towards him, the one in whom God has come near.

This is Good News – good because the one towards whom we turn is good, and news because previously we had believed this turning to be impossible, because we believed that such a move was either pointless, because God would always be too far away, or presumptuous because we, in our sins, might never dare to approach the perfection of God. Dismantling such destructive rumours, Jesus summons us to 'Turn'. 'Turn! Turn! Turn!' he commands, forget all your falsehoods about the remoteness of God, 'Turn! Turn! Turn!' away from the guilt of your failure, 'Turn! Turn! Turn!' to the one who has already drawn near to you.

Through Jesus, God will be present in the villages of Galilee, through him God will touch blinded eyes and skin which is raw; through touch, a womb which bled for twelve long years will be healed. Through a human body, God will be present in Jerusalem: on the donkey, at the meal and yes, even in the shameful, naked agony of the monstrosity of the cross.

Such presence will continue after Jesus has died and risen. 'I am with you always,' he will promise. From now on, the community of followers will be the body of God and the temple of God – a place where it can be said, with the same conviction as by that flaming bush, 'God is here'. And once again, whether in crowds or individual encounter, people will be summoned to turn. As with Moses and Jesus, so in the life of the Church, renewal begins when people respond to the call to turn, to turn towards the God who has already drawn near to them.

This is at the heart of mainline teaching: we always begin with God. The Lutheran Augsburg Confession, the Thirty-nine Articles of Anglicanism, and the Reformed Westminster Confession[1] all begin with descriptions of God. These should not be read as lifeless declarations or legal definitions, but as utterances of profound encounter. Mystics spent hours in Middle Eastern caves, pondering and wrestling with the nature of the divine before such words were ever written down. When renewing our faith, these are the words which must be spoken before all others.

The Shorter Catechism (the bedrock of centuries of Reformed Protestant teaching) begins by stating that the chief end of humanity is to 'glorify God and enjoy him forever'. The foundational moment of Methodism occurred on the evening of 24 May 1738, when John Wesley found his heart strangely warmed. Renewal has always begun through encounter with God.

Presence and Renewal

Why do we need to be reminded of this in the mainline Church? Because, too often, our immediate reflex is to seek renewal by other means: to find the strategy which might lead us to the promised land or the reorganisation which might reinvigorate our work. We give this a spiritual gloss by calling for prayer, but too quickly we embark on whatever activity might see a return of our relevance or our numbers. In doing so, we bypass the need for transformative encounter with God. So often our strategies, drawing inspiration from the world of entrepreneurial leadership, have failed to usher in our renewal because not only do such strategies borrow from the world of Secularism, they also, subtly, reinforce its fundamental assumption that we must do this new thing by ourselves and apart from God.[2]

Furthermore, our renewal must be grounded in divine encounter, because it is through this that we go on to fulfil our primary calling, to embody the presence of God in a world of deep spiritual hunger. Our universal human hunger for God, famously encapsulated in Augustine's prayer, 'You have made us for yourself, O Lord, and our heart is restless until it rests in you', can only be met by a Church which itself has encountered God.

It is intrinsic to our nature as humans to worship some kind of god. James Smith has called our species *Homo liturgicus*, by which he means our fundamental purpose is not to produce, consume, or even think. Rather, we are those who, with all of our being, are made to love and desire that which is beyond ourselves. We are made to worship.[3] Yet too often the objects of our worship can never satisfy our desire – be these the vehicles we drive, the houses which we perpetually improve, the careers we forge or the status we crave. Such idols cannot bear the weight of becoming gods, they collapse under our expectations, and we in turn become shrivelled, diminished and lost. And our hunger remains, for only God is able to be God.

This instinct is present from the earliest stage of life. Sofia Cavaletti, a researcher into the spirituality of young children, tells the story of a 3-year-old girl raised in an atheistic family. One day she asked her father, 'Where did the world come

GOD

from?' He answered in exclusively scientific terms but then added, 'There are some people who say all this comes from a very powerful being and they call him God.' At this the little girl started dancing around the room with joy: 'I knew what you told me wasn't true – it's him, it's him!' The writer Anne Lamott tells a similar story of being raised a devout atheist, but of her frequent backsliding into faith: 'even when I was a child I knew that when I said Hello, someone heard'.[4]

This need for divine presence is further heightened in a secular age which has attempted its radical Disenchantment and found the world still haunted. It has bolted the doors of its reality, the gods have been banished, and yet something mysterious still moves outside the window. God will always make God's presence known beyond the bounds of the Church, but that does not diminish the Church's calling to embody that presence. The need is particularly urgent because as Disenchantment draws nearer to its seeming completion, its incompleteness becomes all the more apparent, and so too does the Church's vocation: to become agents of re-enchantment in a disenchanted age.

Divine Presence in the Mainline Church

A final and critical reason why the Church needs to re-enchant in a secular age particularly applies to the mainline Church, and particularly in relation to the God who announces himself to Moses as 'I am who I am' – that is, God who is unreduced and unconstrained. For the mainline Church has, unwittingly and over many centuries, diminished its account of the 'God who is God', and instead created what the pre-eminent analyst of Secularisation, Charles Taylor, has called a 'pre-shrunk religion'. In doing so, the mainline Church not only made itself vulnerable to Secularisation, but it also created the conditions which made Secularisation possible.[5]

Between the sixteenth and nineteenth centuries, many Protestant churches became wary of excessive fanaticism (a result of the painful history of religious wars), superstition (an outcome of the challenge of science) and even spiritual intimacy (because of our lingering fear that we could never be good enough for God). Out of these anxieties emerged an increasingly dilute and flavourless religion whose god had created the world and its moral laws, but now sat remote in a far-off heaven and restricted himself to acts of general benevolence. To attempt intimacy with such a god was not only futile but also presumptive. But, and this was the worst of all worlds, upon our deaths this distant god suddenly became furiously interested in our lives and would usher us into an afterlife with appropriate punishments and rewards. Unawares, we had created a stern and emotionally distant god, whom we depicted in our imaginations with white hair and a white beard, a god who began to resemble the Greek God Zeus more than the God of Moses or Jesus.

Such a disenchanted god was particularly useful as social elites sought to create a harmonious society, one which incentivised moral conduct among the masses without resorting to the violence and succumbing to the superstitions of the Middle Ages. This religion's tamed and distant deity left behind the spiritual vacuum in which Disenchantment moved from tentative possibility to dominant reality. (This god has evolved more recently, dare it be suggested, into another white-haired, white-bearded semi-deity who is aware of our moral conduct from afar – specifically, the North Pole – and who also motivates good behaviour through a system of appropriate rewards.)

The emaciated 'god of polite society' has, alas, lingered long within the precincts of the mainline. Centuries after the first stirrings of Disenchantment, a survey of Church of Scotland congregations in the 1960s found that 87 per cent of members attended for reasons of respectability and general morality, and that only 13 per cent were primarily motivated by a desire to worship.[6] I think too of the many Scottish parents who would send their children to Sunday School, years after they themselves had stopped going to church; this was not so their offspring might grow into personal faith, but in order that their children might be instructed in, as a parent once put it to me, 'the Ten Commandments and all that stuff'.

This is a serious charge: that we in the mainline Church created the conditions for secular society's Disenchantment, and subsequently played along with it. This is not a charge made lightly, but if we are serious about our renewal then we must face the possibility. I think of a friend who, several years ago, left parish ministry to work full-time for his presbytery. No longer tied to his own congregation, every Sunday he would visit a different church in his presbytery. This turned out to be an utterly dispiriting experience. Sunday after Sunday he encountered worship which felt tired and evoked very little sense of the presence of God. My friend is not a natural cynic, yet if even he was struggling to encounter God in the mainline Church, what hope for those of a more sceptical disposition. Twenty years later, I told this story to one of my friend's successors who affirmed that in his view little had changed. I think too of a Christian organisation which has employed many young Christians in rural areas. It was the organisation's policy that their employees attend their local church, which in every case was a mainline congregation. Many of these young people found adherence to this policy extremely challenging. Though highly impressed by the commitment and hospitality of those in these rural congregations, the young employees regularly complained about experiences of worship which felt pallid and uninspired in comparison to that in their former churches.

Clearly, this is not the universal experience of the mainline. There remain moments when we utter to ourselves, 'Surely God is here.' But too often, over many centuries, we have become places and communities which espouse the muted, predictable, disenchanting and disenchanted god of polite society, rather than the awesome, unlimited, intimate, personal, public, passionate, justice-seeking, risk-inspiring, beguiling and enchanting God of Jesus Christ, the God who is God. Contemporary secularised populations are yearning, sometimes unknowingly, for churches to offer an alternative to the bleakness of Disenchantment; but too often they discover that we have disenchanted alongside them. Too often, when experiencing the worship of the mainline Church, they do not say 'God is here', but instead 'this is boring'. This disconnect between us and God lies at the heart of mainline decline. If we are to be renewed, it is this, before all other things, which we must address.

3

Seek

So how might mainline churches better respond to our calling, to be places and communities of awesome and inspiring divine encounter?

At this point, it may be objected that the presence of God cannot be summoned: that regardless of human petition, God's presence depends entirely on God. In other words, that we cannot ensure the presence of God in our churches, any more than we can ensure the presence of a monarch or an Oscar-winning actor. Even our most fervent prayers may have no effect; presence does not depend on us. However, in one of the great surprises of scripture, we discover this not to be true – but that God not only allows that God be sought, but encourages it.

This is a great mystery: that we humans are summoned to play a vital part in the presence of God. Yet Jesus commands that we 'seek first his kingdom' (Matt. 6:33, NIV) and the psalmist expresses his hope to God that 'all who seek you rejoice and be glad in you' (Ps. 40:16). Though Jesus teaches that the Spirit blows where it chooses (John 3:8), its untamed presence is still responsive to human petition: 'How much more will the heavenly Father give the Holy Spirit to those who ask him?' says Jesus in Luke 11:13.

Julian of Norwich, the medieval mystic, wrote profoundly of her own encounters with God. She testified to the importance of this search, saying it was not the preserve of cloistered monks, nuns and religious enthusiasts but the ordinary undertaking of every human life. But this seeking after God does not somehow put God under the power of our human request, for the original desire for God has its source in God. God wishes to have a relationship with us in which each of us seeks the other. A relationship of love, it seems, could be no other way.[1]

The need for divine presence and encounter was dear to the Church of the early Celts. Continually they invoked the company of 'the sacred three': the Creator, the Christ and the Spirit. 'Christ be beside me, Christ be before me, Christ be above me' expresses the prayer known as St Patrick's Breastplate; or, in the words of another ancient invocation:

> God to surround me,
> God in my speaking,
> God in my thinking.
>
> God in my sleeping,
> God in my waking,
> God in my watching,
> God in my hoping.[2]

With such a desire for divine presence, the Celtic Church spread from Ireland to Scotland, northern England and into Europe, bringing renewal to a medieval Church where faith had begun to wither.

When we seek God, God becomes manifest not only to us, but also to those around. In stories of revival, whether in Cambuslang where I used to minister, or more recently on the Isle of Lewis, the presence of God became intense after Christians – often only a handful of them – continuously *sought* God's presence. When revival came, though, it was not restricted to those who had originally prayed; it became a widespread and communal experience. On Lewis, lights would be seen above buildings from far away, and crowds would walk across fields towards them, often late at night, in the hope that they too might encounter God. This sense of divine presence would be particularly intense during the months of revival but would also continue to linger with those who had experienced it, often for the rest of their lives.[3]

Worship

If divine encounter is essential to Christian renewal, where might it be experienced? We have already spoken of personal and corporate prayer, but there are other possibilities. Rudolph Bultmann was one of the most renowned and controversial New Testament scholars of the twentieth century. Seeking to connect the vocabulary of the Bible with the modern age, he had famously reinterpreted the New Testament's language of 'apocalypse' (which means 'unveiling') as applying to the moment when it was revealed to an individual human being, within their own self, that Jesus is the Christ. In the early 1970s, a young English scholar (and later one of my own teachers), who had spent several years studying and translating Bultmann's work, travelled out to Germany to meet the great man. He and Bultmann (and Bultmann's dogs) went for a walk. After years immersed in Bultmann's thought, the young scholar had one pressing question, and now he had the chance to ask it.

'This personal apocalypse of which you have written ...', he asked, 'when does it actually happen?'

'At 11 o'clock on a Sunday morning, when the church bells ring,' Bultmann immediately replied.

The young man was utterly disappointed with this reply. Was that *it*? The great existential moment of faith was synonymous with Sunday morning worship? Did the great Bultmann have nothing more radical to offer than this – that the gospel of Jesus be reduced to something as apparently mundane as going to church? Did pew-sitting, hymn-singing and sermon-listening truly deserve a description as explosive as 'apocalypse'?

Since that time, New Testament scholars have retained their admiration for Bultmann's intellect and imagination but have rejected most of his conclusions. And yet, as I have pondered on that conversation (in my remembering I never forget Bultmann's dogs), I have often wondered: 'On this, was not Bultmann right?' Perhaps Sunday morning services should indeed be described as an apocalypse? Are they not, after all, an explosive unveiling, a moment when the boundaries of sight are pulled back and we come to believe an outrageous claim: that the one who made us, loved us and redeemed us is truly here?

Annie Dillard, in a sublime essay comparing Sunday worship to a polar expedition, complains that Christians (other than those in 'catacombs') are insufficiently aware of its enormity. 'Does anyone have the foggiest idea what sort of power we blithely invoke?' she asks. 'It is madness to wear ladies' straw hats and velvet hats to church; we should all be wearing crash helmets. Ushers should issue life preservers and signal flares; they should lash us to our pews.'[4]

At its very best, this is my own experience. It is through regular Sunday morning worship, far more than through any evangelistic programme, that I have seen new Christians come into the Church. It is Sunday worship which matters most to members of our congregations. Sunday morning worship should indeed be prepared and led, and participated in, as if it is the very end of the world. It *should* be an apocalypse.

When those 'congregations of difference' were growing in Kendal, I strongly suspect that theirs were worship services with a heightened and expectant sense of God, a meeting with the Almighty who is both other and near. We may dispute some of their teaching (and in later chapters we will), but – for now – let these churches be our teachers: that Sunday morning worship is an encounter with the bigness and intimacy of God, and such an encounter is essential to the renewal of the Church.

The insight that God is not only the object of worship, but present within it, was one of the key impulses which gave birth to the movement known as Contemporary Christian Worship.[5] A friend who belongs to the Vineyard Church, a denomination which has been a pioneer in this movement, reports that when people attend their services after not having been in a church for many years, they very often break down in tears, even during upbeat worship songs. She can find no explanation for this frequently repeated phenomenon other than that, through worship, these individuals are encountering the presence of God. Surely Bultmann was right to call this an apocalypse.

There is no prescribed form of music, nor a particular liturgy which will ensure that our worship is drenched in the presence of God. All forms can inspire, and all can become formulaic. What is critical is that the form speaks to the culture of those who worship. It is also vital that in coming to worship, and in preparing worship, our expectations of God's presence should be heightened; everything else, such as 'busy-ness' and 'programmes', should be darkened, for we need the dark to see the stars. This applies to both those who lead and those who participate. There should be moments, sometimes even long moments, when space is created for encounter, especially when such moments are accompanied by the fear that 'this might not work'. Such moments might involve repeated singing of a chant or worship song; the setting aside of time for silent prayer; proper preparation in the reading of the scriptures; meaningful symbolic action; an expectation of presence during preaching; or sustained attention when we are receiving the bread and wine. We must resist any temptation to keep moving through the 'agenda', or to keep worship palatable and safe. Instead, our worship should regularly allow for moments of participation, expectancy and risk, moments when we might, like Moses, 'turn aside'.

Also, we must give of our best. Worship, the very word deriving from 'worth-ship', is to be as valued as the pearl of great price. Nothing lazy or half-hearted or left-over should be placed on the altar of Sunday morning worship. Liturgy, which literally means work, should be the very best of our labour. We should not offer to God offerings which cost us nothing (2 Sam. 24:24). The writer John Blanchard tells of hours preparing to read the Bible lesson in his home congregation (a part of the service to which we often give little preparation) and of congregants telling him afterwards of an overwhelming sense of divine presence when he had read the lesson. Preachers know too those moments when there is a hush in the congregation, when it feels as if another voice is speaking, when something beyond us is starting to stir. Singers know also the moment when the song has moved beyond words and music and we know ourselves to be singing with the angels. Such moments cannot be ordered up like requests on a radio show, but neither are they unrelated to our seeking, our waiting, our labouring and our yearning. From such moments will our renewal begin.

Wildness

God is never confined to the precincts of the church and must also be sought in the wildest of places. This was the lifelong quest of the famed Scots-American environmentalist John Muir, who was born in Scotland in 1838 before, at the age of 11, emigrating with his family to the United States.[6] Though raised a strict Calvinist, and permitted by his father only to read the Bible, Muir had nevertheless cultivated a love for what he would later call the 'big book' of the cosmos. From a young age, he had been continually entranced by winds, waves and storms. However, it was only through his teachers at the University of Wisconsin that he began to perceive in a new way the dynamic and evolving nature of the universe. This awareness became yet more acute as, a few years later, he recovered from an accident which had almost rendered him blind.

Muir delighted in the realisation that all nature was suffused with the glory of God, that 'every bush is a burning bush', and that the Sermon on the Mount was being continuously preached on every mountain. On first entering California's Yosemite Valley he likened the experience to being born again. Seeking a life which was immersed in nature, Muir lived in remote log cabins and embarked upon long pilgrimages in which he walked barefoot like a latter-day Moses, in order that he might sense the sacredness of the earth with his 'heels' as well as his 'head'. It was in Yosemite, during one stormy night in 1869, that Muir climbed the highest of the trees, a Douglas fir. He lashed himself to its top, and allowed himself to be swayed by the gusts, to feel the terror, to hear other trees crashing around him, to sense the precariousness of his own smallness; and in all these things to know the very presence of God.

This appetite for the thrill of the storm seems to be of divine origin. I often wonder why Jesus chose to walk across the stormy waters of Lake Galilee at night. He could have instantaneously transported himself (as happened in John 6:21) but instead he preferred to walk upon the crashing waves. We are not told his motivation (nor that of Peter who later joins him), but it is difficult to escape the conclusion that Jesus loved being in the wildest of places. It is not simply the wildness which counts, but the experience of being held by a force which is not only bigger than us, but also bigger than the storm. Thus, after the storm has been calmed, the disciples will do something which they have never done before: they will worship Jesus. (Matt. 14:33).

This sense of being held in precarious places is why there is an indelible link between Christian growth and outdoor adventure. It is perhaps no accident that in the nineteenth century the first ever Munroist, Archibald Eneas Robertson, was also a Church of Scotland minister.[7] More recently, Christian adventure camps across the world continue to draw hundreds of people (particularly young people) into an experience of faith and adventure. It is not a coincidence, I believe, that I too came to faith after one such camp: a week of rock climbing on Scotland's Moray coast. There is something sacred in the moment we ascend a ridge, descend a rapid, feel the abseil rope go taut, or traverse an aerial runway. In the strange combination of fear and peace we become more open to the presence of God.

This is also true of pilgrimage: encountering God on long paths, with weary feet and awesome vistas, with a friend or a stranger, or alone. This may mean a day-long walk around Iona or on longer paths, such as Orkney's St Magnus Way, which was recently listed among the world's top ten pilgrimages. For the bolder pilgrim, there is the tantalising draw of even more exotic routes, not least to southern Europe with its Camino de Santiago. Such sacred trails need not, of course, be officially marked. On his 'Poacher's Pilgrimage', ecologist and Quaker Alastair McIntosh walked the west coast of the Isles of Harris and Lewis in Scotland's Outer Hebrides. On the very edge of the British Isles, buffeted by Atlantic gales and surrounded by tumultuous seas, McIntosh frequently encountered sites of 'unusual spiritual intensity', discovering yet again the link between what is wild and what is holy.[8]

For the mainline Church, seeking to rediscover the presence

of God, part of that rediscovery must mean going outside its doors. This may mean travelling to wilder places. In my own parishes, filled with mountains, rivers and lochs, such locations are not hard to find. But this experience is not limited to Highland landscapes. Wildness is wherever we are untethered from the illusion of safety and become exposed to forces beyond our own control. This may mean camping off-grid for several days (apparently it takes two days to lose the rhythms of civilisation), or volunteering as a Street Pastor on late-night city-centre pavements. The Galilean waves were not Jesus' only experience of wildness: he feasted with tax-collectors and outsiders, adding to his reputation as a wine-drinker and glutton; these experiences were, in their own way, as wild as the waves of the lake. All were holy places.

Return to the Sacraments

It is telling that in his search for the origins of the god of 'polite society', Charles Taylor returned to the moment when the early Protestant Reformers had 'disenchanted' the Catholic Mass, making light of its mystery and declaring the bread and wine to be nothing more than that: bread and wine. From this tiny point of origin, says Taylor, over the following centuries Disenchantment was allowed to radiate outwards into every corner of existence.[9]

If we are to re-enchant, we must return to the original source of Disenchantment, to our understanding of the sacraments, and in particular the Eucharist or, depending on our tradition, Communion. Here we might recall that not all Protestant Reformers followed Zurich's Ulrich Zwingli who maintained that the Communion elements were only reminders of the original Last Supper. The understandings of Luther and his disciple Melanchthon were not far from the earlier Catholic understanding: that the bread and wine were somehow transformed into the very body and blood of Christ (any other understanding had been imposed by the devil, wrote Luther, in typically robust terms). But even that arch-iconoclast

John Calvin taught that there was a 'real presence' when we celebrated Communion. Thus to re-enchant the Eucharist or Communion is an authentically Protestant move.

We must also go beyond the officially named sacraments to reclaim the sacramental potential of all things, to affirm along-side Barbara Brown Taylor that 'regarded properly, anything can become a sacrament, by which I mean an outward and visible sign of inward and spiritual connection'.[10] Many of the gifts we will later explore in this book possess this innate sacramental quality; for just as we encounter God in worship (which is our deepest centre) and wildness (which is our furthest edge), so an awareness of the sacramental potential of all things enables us to encounter God in every place between. And this possibility includes, despite our historic disenchantments, the life of the mainline Church.

4

Saved

Six miles north of the Speyside town of Grantown, beside the road which snakes across the Dava Moor, there sits a boulder. For over 100 years, it has displayed the same two words ...
'Jesus Saves'.

Rumour is that the stone was first painted by a returning missionary. What first inspired this person? And why those particular words? Over the last century, on several occasions, the paints and brushes have been passed on. Each successive keeper of the stone has chosen to stay relatively unknown, preferring that the focus remain on those two words: 'Jesus Saves'.

There are three congregations in Grantown-on-Spey: Baptist, Church of Scotland and Episcopalian. In which of these congregations did the stone-keepers worship? I had always presumed it was the Baptists, and recent research has proved my assumption correct. 'Jesus Saves', I'd assumed, was 'their kind of thing'. Many mainliners, if we're honest, find this kind of slogan a little embarrassing, a little too gauche. Our spirituality prefers to speak of 'God with us', or 'Jesus as friend', or 'Jesus of the outsiders'. 'Jesus Saves' feels a little too, well, extreme.

However, 'Jesus Saves' needs to be reclaimed in the mainline. It is the strongest antidote to that false god we need to banish, the tamed anaemic god we met in Chapter 2, the 'god of polite society'. We need these words to overcome our historic instinct for keeping God at a safe distance; 'Jesus Saves' proclaims not only that God comes near, but also that God, in Jesus, does something. Not something irrelevant, but that he changes us, and rescues us from some kind of plight. But we do not like to be rescued. We prefer that religion does not disturb our decorum or our sense of self-sufficiency: roadside slogans should be left to the Baptists. However, we in the mainline need 'Jesus Saves' precisely because it upsets our complacency and fear of discomfort. We need to reclaim the message of that boulder on the Dava Moor.

A Wider Salvation

Before fully reclaiming 'Jesus Saves', though, we do have to expand its meaning, for part of our resistance to 'Jesus Saves' spirituality is indeed well-founded. It is resistance to an overly narrow understanding of what these words mean.

When first coming to faith I was working in our local super-market. One of the women who worked in the delicatessen was a churchgoer and heard about my conversion. One day she came up to me, not with delight but more with the efficiency of someone sorting the Brie from the Danish Blue. 'Oh, I didn't know you were saved,' she declared, looking me up and down, before turning around and walking off. I hated that. It was such a cold encounter; it felt like a categorisation. And I had never heard that language before, it felt like insiders' jargon, a code for identifying who was in and who was out.

The Bible has a much wider range of meaning when it speaks of being saved. The Old Testament rarely refers to an afterlife, and yet it frequently refers to being 'saved' or to the related idea of 'salvation'. To be saved in the Old Testament means to be liberated from slavery, delivered from enemies, healed from disease, rescued from danger, and reconciled with God. In the New Testament, saving is still about being rescued from perilous places – from shipwreck, enemies, darkness, alienation and corruption. There is also, through the death and resurrec-tion of Jesus, a heightened emphasis on the forgiveness of sins and our resurrection into the life to come. Salvation is about being brought into an eternal relationship, a love affair even, whose effects are utterly transformative, and which will never be broken; not by our failures, nor by our death.

In Greek and Hebrew the words 'save' and 'salvation' share the same root but are often translated into a range of different

English words: deliver, heal or rescue are the most common of these. Thus, we often miss how much saving is going on in the scriptures. At root, the word for 'saved' means 'brought to a spacious place', which I like a lot. One final connection should be noted: the Hebrew 'to save', *yasha*, leads directly to the name Yeshua, which we translate as 'Jesus', meaning 'YHWH saves'. Thus, 'Jesus Saves', translated into Hebrew, literally means 'YHWH saves saves'. 'Saving' is at the very heart of who Jesus is.

The Carols Were Right

Several years ago I was involved in leading an Advent workshop whose intention was to show that, by importing a cartload of Victorian romanticism and too many references to Easter, Christmas carols had corrupted Christmas. The workshop involved covering the walls of whichever room we were in with large sheets of paper, on which were printed all the episodes of the Christmas story: Elizabeth and Zechariah, Gabriel and Mary, the Manger, the Magi, Herod, the flight to Egypt. All the stories were there. Participants were given a photocopy of a well-known carol, a pair of scissors and some glue. They were to cut out individual lines of the carol, then stick these on to whichever Christmas episode it had originated from. So 'offspring of a virgin's womb' might be stuck on to the sheet containing Matthew 1:23, 'Look! The virgin shall conceive and bear a son.'

On the wall there were two additional sheets of paper, entitled 'Fanciful Speculation' and 'Not Christmas'. The first of these was to be a repository for any line in a carol which could not be biblically justified, and the second was intended to catch all those carols which were jumping ahead to Easter.

By the end of the workshop, there were four discoveries:

1   Christmas carols do contain a pile of unwarrantable nonsense: 'Snow had fallen, snow on snow', 'No crying he makes' and, as a description of childbirth, 'How silently, how silently, the wondrous gift is given.'

2 Carols crowd around a few select Christmas verses, in particular Luke 2:7: 'she laid him in a manger' and, most popular of all, Luke 2:14: 'Glory to God in the highest heaven, and on earth peace among those whom he favours!'
3 Many Christmas episodes are neglected: the stories of Elizabeth and Zechariah, Simeon and Anna, the massacre of the infants (although present in a few older carols) and the flight to Egypt.
4 The 'Not Christmas' sheet was empty.

I was slightly upset at that last result ... had participants not followed their instructions? Had they not spotted when incarnation morphed into atonement? Surely they had recognised that 'born that man no more may die', or 'Christ the redeemer is here', has only a little to do with Christmas? But no, they had been more perceptive than me, locating several references to 'saving' and 'salvation' in the Christmas story. They identified verses such as Matthew 1:21: 'you are to name him Jesus, for he will save his people from their sins', or Luke 1:71: 'that we would be saved from our enemies', or Luke 1:77: 'to give knowledge of salvation'.

Those last two references come from the longest passage in the whole Christmas narrative – the song of Zechariah, father of John the Baptist. His joyous hymn celebrates the many facets of salvation: being rescued from enemies, sins being forgiven, the favour of God, light dawning on those in darkness, being led into the way of peace.

The carols, it turned out, were not wrong. Salvation is inherent to the meaning of Christmas, but it is a broad view of salvation: forgiveness, rescue, enlightenment and peace. And as salvation is inherent to Christmas, it is inherent to the whole life of Jesus, not just its end. Thus John the Baptist proclaims at the start of Jesus' ministry: 'Behold the lamb of God who takes away the sin of the world' (John 1:29, ESV) as a description of the whole of Jesus' life, not only its end.

When it was recently proposed to a gathering of ministers that 'Jesus Saves' needs to be reclaimed, a colleague protested that the term is too vague. 'Saved from what?', he asked. 'Saved from everything we need to be saved from' is probably the best Biblical answer. The Biblical definition of salvation is broad, inviting our imagination to ask, 'In this place, in this time, what does it mean to be saved?' Depending on where we are, salvation may mean deliverance from spiritual darkness, violent threats, ill-health, environmental degradation, patriarchy, personal guilt, debilitating work situations or hostile neighbours – all are encompassed within scripture's wide-boundaried account of salvation. Once we recognise the whole breadth of saving and salvation, we are at last ready to reclaim the words 'Jesus Saves', and reclaim them we must if we are to be saved from our bloodless, inoffensively 'polite-ified' and secularised image of God.

Faith

In the scriptures, 'Jesus Saves' is closely entwined with a human response: faith. This kind of faith is, fundamentally, an act of trust, a new way of seeing and an openness to whatever new possibility God might bring to pass. In the Gospels, faith strengthens our endurance; drops stretchers through roofs; lunges for Jesus in a hostile crowd; demands that Jesus heal the people we love; and moves prayer from the monotony of empty phrases to the truest yearnings of the soul. Even in small quantities, faith is effective and dares to trust that even in the most tangled mess, somehow Jesus might hold all of it and all of us.

Faith is the human move, in the dance of divine salvation. 'By grace you have been saved through faith' says the letter to the Ephesians (Eph. 2:8); 'Have faith in the Lord Jesus Christ, and you will be saved' says Paul in Acts (Acts 16:31, my own translation).[1] Once we gain a glimpse of salvation and the God who saves, we also start to grow in faith: the kind of faith which leads to us being renewed.

Testify

In the scriptures there is an essential link between salvation and being saved. There is also an essential link between salvation and telling stories. In my first year at High School, I was introduced to Scripture Union (usually abbreviated to 'SU'), and a style of faith I hadn't previously encountered. The leaders of our SU group were from our local Baptist church and there was something different about them. I didn't always agree with the dogmatic answers they gave to my most persistent questions, but they had an enthusiasm and passion which I found inspiring, and despite my semi-heretical awkwardness they allowed me to belong (which, in the first year at secondary school, is a very precious commodity).

One Sunday evening the group was invited along to our leaders' church. One of the elders was giving his testimony. I hadn't even heard the word 'testimony' before. This was entirely new, I wasn't used to ordinary non-ministerial people speaking for so long in services, and telling stories of such a personal nature. This man, I can still remember the brown suit he was wearing, had been seriously ill; doctors had found in him an incurable tumour, the 'size of a melon'. He told us the story of when his condition had worsened and it didn't look as if he would make it; but his wife had prayed, the pastor had prayed, the whole church had prayed. Then something remarkable had happened, he began to feel better. After a few days of getting better, he was taken for an x-ray. The results were stunning: the impossible had happened, his 'incurable' tumour had disappeared. The doctors had never seen anything like it.

I can remember that there was nothing showy about this man's delivery, he spoke with a kind of quietened awe; what had happened to him was so remarkable that he had no need to over-dramatise. That night, in the telling, it was as if he revisited again the sheer miracle of being alive. 'The cancer might well return,' he said, 'but tonight I am simply glad to be here.' After he spoke, the pastor shared some of his own memories of this man's illness, and then added, almost as an afterthought, 'perhaps one of the biggest reasons you were healed was so you could come and tell your story tonight'. Maybe it was. Stories are that important.

For these Baptists, this storytelling seemed like a commonplace: something bad or unusual happened, people prayed, something remarkable happened, and then you told the story. The psalms are full of this: 'I will tell of all your wonderful deeds' (Ps. 9:1), 'I have told the glad news of deliverance' (Ps. 40:9) or 'I will declare your greatness' (Ps. 145:6).

In this, we shy mainliners have much to learn. For storytelling is not merely an enjoyable hobby, or a 'slot' in the service. It is vital to our renewal. John Hayward is a mathematician who, for many years, has applied his skills to better understand the growth of the Church. After years of analysing numbers and modelling sophisticated systems, he has developed a thesis at whose heart is the following key idea: 'A growing Church needs enthusiasts who tell others.' If the enthusiasts become discouraged, if they stop telling their stories, then the Church will cease to grow. But if they are truly renewed by God, they tell their story, others will hear and become enthusiastic storytellers themselves. Stories are that important.

So here, as a start, are five stories of salvation.

On My Knees

Arriving in India in 1994, employed as a Christian youth worker, I felt like an impostor. Maybe it was the shock of being in a new country, perhaps it was the pressure of being paid to believe, but my faith no longer felt real. For months, I prayed and prayed, but found no relief: seemingly unforgiven, doubt-ridden, far from home, defrauding a church who were paying me to be someone I wasn't. I felt utterly miserable and alone.

I will never forget the day this changed: it was in a crowded church in a town called Nedumangad. I was visiting with my great friend Jacob, the diocesan youth worker, who, as part of his work, would speak at different congregations each Sunday. Every week, being that he was clergy, and me being almost clergy, we'd be brought to the front of the church and made to sit at the front, facing the congregation. With this privileged position came an expectation I dreaded: during the Eucharist, which came at the end of every service, the clergy would be expected to kneel for a far greater part of the liturgy than the rest of the congregation. This was always agony: my unpractised Presbyterian thighs were unused to such long periods of prostration. Even worse, in this particular congregation in Nedumangad, there were no carpets; the floor was solid concrete.

And so, on this particular Sunday, after an already long service, I found myself kneeling for what seemed like hours, on a hard hard floor, my knees in pain, my legs burning and, if this were possible, my soul even sorer. All the usual doubts were raging, the same sense of inadequacy, of sin and, above all, the feeling that God knew what a hypocrite I was and would soon be done with me. The liturgy continued in the local language, Malayalam, which meant that after the first few minutes I lost all sense of how far through we were. I remember praying, 'God, I hate this, I am not sure if I believe any of this, I am not sure if you are there, and even if you are, I think you might have given up on me, and these people think I am some kind of super-Christian, kneeling here at the front, and I am so, so, so sore.' And then it came. Like a moment of light. I suddenly knew – I can't explain this, I simply knew – that two verses I had read that morning – 'once you were alienated from God and were enemies in your minds because of your evil behaviour *but now* he has reconciled you' (Col. 1:21–22, NIV) – were about me. There were no miraculous confirmations, I just knew. That moment was an epiphany which sustained me through the rest of that year in India: one of the hardest years of my life but also one of the best years of my life.

There were two releases that day. The first was a release from guilt. I knew with renewed faith that somehow I had been brought into the death of Jesus, in which God had taken all the sin of the world into God's own self, that human beings like me might be made right again: I felt unburdened and loved. The only language I can find to express this experience is that it felt like light had flooded my inner world. The second release was a release from the terror of a god whom all of us have known at some point in our lives: god as the perpetually unsatisfied parent, the disapproving teacher, the god who, for the slightest reason, will condemn and abandon us, and with whom there is precious little hope of reconciliation. That day, on my aching knees, I was released from that miserable god, a god who stayed away for a long time afterwards. Instead, I met again the God of abundant, overwhelming light. The God to whom Jesus pointed when he announced, 'Good news!'

Oh how we need this sense of God in the mainline because, despite our more reasonable god, we still carry huge burdens of inadequacy and guilt. This is not addressed through attempting to make our god even more amenable and agreeable. We sense the inauthenticity of such a move and inherently distrust it. Rather, we are called to inhabit, with renewed conviction, salvation as the stunning and essential gift of forgiveness, and the revelation of God who is with us and for us. Always.

On the Glacier

In 1997 I found myself in the French Alps, being taught to ski alongside my great friend Matt. We were both relative novices and Matt hated this. He had just left the Royal Marines where he'd risen from raw recruit to becoming one of the best in his unit. The feeling of being a beginner again was not one he enjoyed.[2]

Late one morning, our ex-military instructor had clearly decided that too many well-groomed pistes were spoiling us; we needed to be tested in an altogether more challenging environment. High up on the mountain, skiing under a rope and a warning sign, he led us on to the resort's glacier (in hindsight, of course, we should never have done this). At one point, he plunged his pole through the snow to reveal the mouth of a crevasse. 'Always avoid cracks like this,' he warned, while – it seemed – very much *not* avoiding 'cracks like this'. After twenty minutes the terrain was becoming far too treacherous and it

was time to return to the relative safety of the piste. This neces-
sitated an extremely tight turn on steep and icy snow. If this
were not already frightening, just below us was the edge of an
ice-cliff, plunging hundreds of feet on to the rocks below. We
beginners were terrified, but our instructor, seemingly unper-
turbed, turned and headed for home. Matt volunteered to go
next. To my horror, halfway through his turn, his skis suddenly
slipped out from underneath him. Landing on his side, he began
sliding inexorably towards the drop below. With a look of
terror on his face, frantically hitting his pole against what was
now sheet ice, Matt looked doomed. I was convinced we would
lose him. And then, miraculously, just inches from oblivion,
one of Matt's skis found a tiny patch of soft snow, just enough
to stop his fall.

Feeling utter relief, we could only laugh as Matt stood up,
quickly altered his facial expression from terrified to noncha-
lant, and declared: 'That's the fifth time I've almost died.' For
the rest of the day, Matt would tell anyone he met about the
ice-cliff, the futile stabbing of his pole, the tiny patch of miraculously soft snow: the fifth time that he had almost died. Ever
since, he has needed little prompting to retell that story – or
indeed to recount the other four occasions when he almost met
his demise.

After hearing Matt's story, any reasonable hearer will raise
questions: 'That was only a small patch of snow ... small patches
of snow are everywhere on French glaciers, why attribute their
fortunate placement to God?' and 'What about all the other
skiers who dug their poles in and whose falls were not broken,
leading to fatality?' Matt's story doesn't gloss over these kinds
of questions but, rather, it does the opposite: it provokes
them. By telling stories of life and salvation, we cannot but
ask questions about the times when salvation is considerably
harder to discern. I write these words in the painful shadow
of two such stories of sudden and inexplicable loss. We have
two broad possibilities: silence all stories, or narrate all stories.
The invitation of faith is, I believe, to choose the latter; to insist
that life is 'storied', with stories which confirm our faith, and
the stories which challenge it. I think of the psalmists who bore

witness, saying: 'My mouth will tell of your righteous acts, of your deeds of salvation all day long' (Ps. 71:15), and who also asked the most raw of questions: 'My God, my God, why have you forsaken me?' (Ps. 22:1).

We have a choice: the unnarrated path of silence with its apparently defensible god, or the way of stories which both confirm and challenge our faith. It is towards the second of these that we must move in the mainline, to rediscover God whose presence is woven into all our living, with all its affirmations and all its questions; to tell stories of the God who does not fit into tidy categories, the God who always retains the freedom to be God.

Boxing Day

Mark is a self-employed painter who got ill every Boxing Day. *Really* ill, not-able-to-move ill, excruciating pain-all-down-the-front-of-his-body ill. Every year he'd enjoy Christmas, and then on Boxing Day the illness would hit him. Being self-employed, holidays were rarities for Mark, and this sickness meant yet another year of wasted holiday, of being ill in bed rather than spending time with his family. He'd been to doctors, had dozens of tests, but no cure had been found. On some Boxing Days, the illness was so bad that Mark would be taken into Hairmyres hospital in East Kilbride, and lie for hours on a hospital bed, just waiting for that year's bout of sickness to be over.

One December, on a post-Christmas run, I'd gone further than expected, so phoned Anna to say I'd be late back. 'You're not far from Hairmyres,' she said, 'you should go and see Mark.' I wasn't sure, I didn't know when visiting time was, and I didn't think muddy running gear would be welcome in a hospital ward. 'Just go,' Anna urged.

Finding Mark's bed, I sat next to him, only for a doctor to approach and ask me to leave since visiting time was over. 'I'm a Church of Scotland minister,' I told him. Slightly concerningly, given my utterly shambolic state, he instantly believed me, and so I stayed. Mark told me how he was doing, how much pain he was still in, and I listened, wishing I could help. I asked if I could pray for him. At this point, I should point out that Mark is not a churchgoer. He has a strong belief in a higher power, but not one who is specifically Christian. But Mark seemed to think prayer was worth trying. Laying a hand on his stomach, I voiced a short prayer, asked for Mark to get better, and said Amen. Before leaving, I almost apologised to Mark, sorry that I'd done so little to help.

However, something remarkable happened. After that prayer, Mark got better and was soon discharged from hospital. The following December, something happened on Boxing Day which hadn't happened for years: Mark didn't become ill. And neither did he get sick the next year, or the year after that.

Every year in late December I expected to hear that Mark's run of good health was over, that he was back in hospital. But instead I'd hear the opposite: he'd stayed well throughout the holidays. Every time we spoke about this, Mark seemed to have more faith than me. If I'm honest, I often attributed his recovery after prayer to coincidence, and didn't expect it to last. Mark had no such doubts: he felt he'd got better because we'd prayed, and he fully anticipated that the following Boxing Day he'd be fine. In the scriptures, being healed is being saved. And in the Gospels, this is linked to faith, not how often you go to church.

Alastair Cram

Born in Perth in 1904, Alastair Cram, a lawyer and accomplished mountaineer, had realistic ambitions of climbing Mount Everest in 1939, before his plans were scuppered by the outbreak of the Second World War. Joining the army, he was posted to North Africa and, after an attack in November 1941, was captured by the German Afrika Corps. This, however, was not the end of Alastair Cram's war, but the beginning of an incredible chapter, one for which he is still remembered.

In Allied Prisoner-of-War camps, most prisoners came to accept their captivity. This was not without good reason. Camp conditions were considerably better when there was a tacit understanding with the guards that no-one would try to escape. Many prisoners embarked on projects or learned skills which served them well in later life. Despite this, in any camp there would always remain a stubborn group of men who were determined to get out, and no-one was more determined than Alastair Cram. Incredibly, over the next three-and-a-half years he would manage to escape from captivity on no fewer than twenty-one separate occasions.[3]

Why was Cram so intent on escaping? First, he saw the debilitating results of incarceration, its degrading effect on the dignity and the will. He described escape as 'a need, a spiritual necessity'. The escape itself was also a spiritual experience: the exhilaration of the first few seconds outside the wire; the hours and days evading capture and the sensation of not being alone, of being guided by a mysterious presence. He experienced the 'unspeakable heightening of perception' as he became wholly aware of every sight and every sound, and even (and this was a surprise) the relief of the first few moments of being recaptured, of no longer having to hide. Then, for Alastair, back in custody and often in solitary confinement, sometimes having been beaten, there would be bleak despair before his deep yearning for liberation would once again return.

After some of his escapes, Alastair had been recaptured within minutes; sometimes he remained free for weeks. No matter the devastation of each recapture, he kept trying. Then in April 1945, during a forced march, he used a rest break to hurriedly disguise himself as a civilian. Walking past his guards, then hiking several days across mountains which reminded him of his beloved Cairngorms, he was eventually found by the advancing US Army. At last, Alastair Cram was free.

After the war, Cram became a judge in British-ruled Kenya. During the Mau Mau rebellion, he was greatly disturbed to see that many of the prisoners in his court had clearly been tortured. Further investigation revealed a horrific network of camps, in which local officials, loyal to the British, held rebel suspects in brutal conditions. Alastair wrote a damning judgement on one of those officials, not only condemning the camps, but also the complicity and collusion of the colonial authorities.

Those same authorities sought to ignore and discredit his findings and, despite Alastair's objections, these were cast aside as the British sought to hold on to power. It would take until 2013 for a small number of Mau Mau prisoners to receive any kind of justice. It is striking, though, that a man who fought so hard to escape prison himself also fought equally determinedly to free others who were unjustly and brutally held.

Salvation as liberation is an understanding that goes back to the Old Testament and the story of the exodus. Alastair Cram's story of determined liberation is thus a salvation story. And yet, remarkably, in the 400-page biography of his life there is very little mention of whether Alastair professed faith. Alastair's wife, Isabel, was an indomitable stalwart of Church of Scotland life, but of Alastair's own faith almost nothing is known. However, such connections must be remade, for our faith is for all those who yearn for release, inspired by the liberative zeal of God who sets the prisoners free.

There is also something important in Alastair Cram's belief, while he was imprisoned, in a life beyond the wire. Charles Taylor comments that one of the features of Secularism is that we have lost our sense of any world beyond this one, and that we have reduced ourselves to a kind of middled existence, in which we make do with this world, and in this limited framework we do the best we can.[4] But in the New Testament, there is a new and radical insistence that salvation also means salvation to a world beyond this one. To believe in such an existence is frightening; such an expansive hope leads us to decisions which sacrifice the comforts of now, yet the early Christians courageously believed in this. In the mainline Church, despite our caution, we are summoned to believe in the same: in a heaven without death, of renewed bodies, and wiped-away tears, of a feast to which we have been invited and of being, at last, truly free.

Alison, Rob and Rima

My friend Alison is the UNESCO[5] Professor of Refugee Integration at Glasgow University. She and her husband Robert have given their lives to welcoming refugees and challenging governments to meet their international obligation to provide sanctuary to those who seek asylum. In the late 2000s, Alison and Robert fostered Rima, a young Eritrean refugee. Somehow this unaccompanied 16-year-old girl had managed to cross the Sahara Desert, the Mediterranean Sea, the European Continent and the English Channel until she found herself in Glasgow. There, she sought leave to remain in the United Kingdom, and thus endured the psychological and physical exhaustion of the UK immigration process, a process which Rob and Alison, through bitter experience, knew only too well. During this time Rima was in serious danger of being taken to an immigration removal centre by the UK Home Office, so Alison and Robert arranged for Rima to stay safe at various locations around the city. If necessary, this would mean that if there was a dawn raid then officials would not find her.

In those early years, of what Rima called her 'joining-ment', welcome was expressed through meals, drink and clothing, loss, laughter and the prayers of Alison, Robert and Rima's friends. 'Prayer was such an important part of that time,' remembers Alison today. In order to help Rima stay connected to her roots, Alison and Robert, both passionate linguists, had begun learning Tigrinya, one of the nine Eritrean languages; they also accompanied Rima to many events which were held by the Eritrean community in Glasgow. Unbeknown to them, at a First Communion service in 2011, a video was taken of the ceremony and of the guests. One woman, with a visa to return to Eritrea, had taken a copy of the video back to her home village. She played the tape to a friend, pointing out the Scottish couple making brave (but not perhaps totally expert) attempts at Eritrean dancing, and also Rima, the Eritrean girl whom they had fostered. 'Rima! Rima!' said the neighbour. 'I know her, she is related! Her mother and sister are actually here now, in our village.' Running round to another house, bursting through the door, she announced: 'You will never believe who I've just seen!'

Rima's mum and sister were stunned. Not having heard from Rima for years and knowing the numbers who perished when attempting to flee, they had presumed the worst. Immediately they rushed back to the first woman's house, demanding to see the video. 'Like all the best resurrection stories,' says Alison, 'it was spread through the gossip of women.'

Word was sent back to Glasgow, and Rima was told 'your family are alive, they saw you on video, they're in Eritrea'. As soon as they could, Alison, Robert and Rima booked flights to Sudan (then a safe country in which to meet) and, a few months later, found themselves being driven to a residential property on the outskirts of Khartoum. Entering the house, climbing the stairs, and coming into a large, upstairs room, they were overwhelmed by an outpouring of undiluted and unrestrained joy. There was wailing, and laughing, and occasional talking, but above all there was joy, wave after wave of joy. Eventually Rima's grandfather stood up to make a speech. 'For year upon year', he said, 'I prayed and I prayed. And every time I prayed, things only got worse ... but today ... today ... salvation has come to my house.'

I love Rima's story: a story of rice and cloth and blankets and water; of community, belonging, realism, determination, safety, prayers, escapes and joy. It is a story which encapsulates the breadth of what Rima's grandfather, and the Bible, call salvation.

Back to the Moor

Salvation stories are not formulaic. They are not tame. Neither are they always especially religious. But they are stories of what actually happened, of how convention was defied, risks were taken, prayers were said, people waited, miracles unfolded and, in the end, life won out over death. Though we tell them too rarely, such stories are not alien to the mainline.

Recently, on contacting the Baptists of Grantown-on-Spey, I

was told something more of the story of the Dava Stone. Some time during the 1950s and 1960s, the road across the Moor was due to be diverted, but the Dava Stone stood right in the middle of its proposed new route. Being far too heavy to move, the council planned to blow it up – until a Church of Scotland minister, and local councillor, insisted that under no circumstances was this to be done. Instead, the Stone, though having to be split in two, would be moved to the side of the new road. Not only within the Baptist Church, but also within the Church of Scotland it transpired, was the value of the Stone's message understood. Indeed, over the years, when the paint has faded or even been vandalised, it turns out that volunteers from all the local churches have ensured its restoration. 'Jesus Saves' belongs to the whole of the Church, including the mainline.

5

Me

The Great Sins of Presbyterianism

Growing up within Scottish Presbyterianism it was assumed I would never murder. The great prohibitions were of sins I would be much more likely to commit:

- Lying.
- Stealing (albeit at the Woolworth's Pic 'n' Mix).
- Being dirty (which was to do with dirty jokes or mentioning certain body parts).
- Being selfish.

Those four great prohibitions – along with the great injunction to work hard – form the backbone of Presbyterian morality, a morality which is widely shared across the mainline. It is the last of these which has proved to be the most troublesome in the secular edge: 'Don't be selfish'.

In Chapter 1 we noted that Secularisation has consisted of two significant movements: Disenchantment (there is no God), and the turn to the self. This turn to the self, sometimes abbreviated simply to 'the turn', is a turn away from living by external roles such as 'dutiful child, and loving and caring spouse' and towards inner feelings and a deep connection with our own experience.[1] For sociologists Paul Heelas and Linda Woodhead, the turn to the self is not only the 'defining cultural development of modern western culture',[2] but is also, even more than the loss of belief, the single biggest cause of decline in mainline churches. In their study of religious belief and participation in the northern English town of Kendal (see Chapter 1), they encountered numerous individuals who left the Church because 'you don't get anything out of it'. One woman had left the Church and taken up transcendental meditation because she now believed in 'the spirituality within each individual', not a creed likely to gain unanimous acceptance in the average main-line congregation.

This is a huge change, even from my childhood in the 1970s. I could imagine the reaction if I had announced as a young boy that I intended to 'live in deep connection with the unique experiences of my inner self' – 'SELFISH!' would have been the instant admonition. Churches remain on the alert against any cultural move which smacks of 'individualism', 'religious consumerism', an obsession with personal authenticity or 'the myth of self-actualisation'. I recently heard a preacher declare that 'be yourself' is the 'worst advice you can ever give to anyone'.

There are two reasons why we should resist such anti-individualism. The first is pragmatic, for there is unlikely to be any going back to the old era of collective thinking. And, even if there were, would it be so much better than our new dispensation? Would we wish to return to the forced spiritual conformity of the earlier era with, to quote Taylor, 'its hypocrisy, spiritual stultification, inner revolt against the Gospel, the confusion of faith and power, and even worse'?[3]

The second reason to question our reflexive mainline anti-individualism (for, at its worst, that is what it becomes) is to ask if the turn to the self is quite so inherently unchristian? And furthermore, what harm might we have done to ourselves, both as congregations and as individuals, through our insistence that joy comes though putting 'Jesus first, Others second, Yourself last'?[4]

The Ladies Who Made Lunch

In my previous congregation, there was a particular moment when this question felt sharper than any other. It would happen on the Sundays when, as a congregation, we would eat lunch together. On these occasions, with absolute regularity, during the last verse of the last hymn half-a-dozen worshippers would rise from their seats, walk discreetly towards the front of the church, and exit through a door which led to the adjacent hall. These were the people who were in charge of preparing lunch and they were almost always women.

In what I say next, I am very anxious to show that I honour these women. Our church could not have functioned without them; they served the lunch with a lot of laughter, were always the first to volunteer, and I personally could not have survived without their friendship and support.

But I did wonder about their role because I knew these women's stories. They had lived almost their whole lives giving to others. Some had left school aged 14, so they could look after the house, their parents and their male siblings. After marriage, they had given up full-time employment to bring up children and look after the home, sometimes also working in part-time jobs to supplement the household income. When grandchildren had been born, these women had provided much of the childcare so their own children could continue to work. These were women who had spent their lives looking after parents, siblings, husbands, children and grandchildren. And now, whenever we had a lunch, the church was saying: 'Could you also look after us?'

I wondered about the cost of this. Occasionally the resentment was barely below the surface. Some were fed up with always being the one whom everyone else relied on. Even if they weren't resentful, once you came to know these women and saw beneath the cheerful public face, you became aware of how much this had cost them. You were aware of the opportunities lost, that cherished dreams had often been sacrificed to enable the dreams of others. And the Church had colluded in this, as indeed it has colluded with so much which has been extremely harmful to women.

And what of those women who were no longer in the Church? What of the many women who have left mainline churches since the 1960s because they were furious at the institution's indifference to their aspirations, those who resolved, like the Scottish national poet Liz Lochhead, that never in a month of Sundays would they go back?[5]

Neglect, even hatred, of the self has too often been a corner-stone of the Church's teaching on what it is to be a follower of Jesus. We emphasise love of neighbour and downplay the second part of the commandment which assumes that 'we love ourselves'. We are taught to mistrust the self, for the 'heart is devious above all else' (Jer. 17:9). How often have we heard sermons on Martha and Mary which immediately seek to defend Martha's industry and downplay Jesus' insistence that Mary had chosen the 'better part' (Luke 10:38–42)? When newcomers appear in our midst, we leave them alone just long enough not to appear desperate, before asking them to volunteer for the coffees, the welcome team or the creche. As comedian Milton Jones has observed: churches are like giant helicopters, if you hang around too long, you get sucked into the rotas.

The residue of this has sunk deep. This continued anti-self teaching and, more critically, the behaviours we model and applaud, have taught us not to value ourselves. We do not think that we, as individuals, are worth too much attention or care. With the poet Pádraig Ó Tuama, we might say, 'It can be diffi-cult to be kind to yourself. Even writing those words, I feel awkward, as if kindness towards myself is a luxury.'[6]

The True Self

Before addressing a better response to 'the turn', we must first examine it more closely. Though purporting to elevate the self above all external authorities, there is actually a second actor at work. 'The turn' may not be so individually empowering as it might seem for, as Charles Taylor has also observed, the contemporary self is only a self in relation to others.[7] We can only be a self if others validate the self which we have become.

This is illustrated in that great drama of the subjective turn, the reality TV show. Whether in a house or on an island, in a competition to sing or bake, a key feature (indeed cliché) of these shows is the individual 'journey'. Contestants are not only judged as to their charm or talent but by the extent to which they have discovered themselves over the lifetime of the show. And note the second actor at work here. This is not solely about the contestant, but also about the audience. If the audience approves of the individual's journey, she or he will advance to next week's show, but if the audience disapproves then eviction ensues. There is no such thing as autonomous self. Within Secularisation, we are always the self in relation to another.[8]

And this is where the gospel speaks.

Because yes, the gospel is resistant to a self which seeks its deepest identity in the approval of the crowd (Luke 6:26), or in misleading inner desires (Eph. 4:22). However, the 'new self' (Eph. 4:24) is rooted in God. The gospel affirms the self-in-relation, not in relation to our cultural mores nor even the Church's validation nor our internal delusions (and such things do exist), but in relation to God who loves without condition and conforms us to God's own image.

One of the greatest teachers in this area, the Trappist monk Thomas Merton, repeatedly contrasted the 'true-self in God', with the 'false-self of egocentric desire'. Of the false-self, he wrote in the starkest terms: it is the person of deluded ambition who can never truly exist; but the gift of God is 'the true inner self, the true indestructible and immortal person, the true "I"'.[9]

The former Archbishop of Canterbury Rowan Williams has a theory which he began developing after meeting Archbishop Desmond Tutu – that there are two kinds of egoists in the world: 'There are egoists that are so in love with themselves that they have no room for anybody else and there are egoists that are so in love with themselves that they make it possible for everybody else to be in love with themselves.'[10]

This second kind of egoist is the 'new self' of Ephesians, or the 'true-self' of Thomas Merton. It is this self whom Jesus affirms when he commands us to 'love your neighbour as yourself' (Mark 12:31). It is this self who is manifest in the self-acceptance which Jesus models in his great prayer in John 17: a prayer which is a continuous dance of I, You and Them – Jesus, the Father and the community. Throughout this prayer, Jesus refers to himself on a remarkable sixty-nine occasions. But this is not self-obsessed egoism, but instead a sense of self which continuously leads to the Father and others. This sense of the true-self is not only seen in Jesus, but in the teaching of Paul (his affirmation of the 'new self' in Ephesians or the anguished internal wrestling of Romans 7); or in the writings of Augustine (whose highly personal 'journey', *Confessions*, is sometimes regarded as the first autobiography); or in the writings of the great medieval mystic Julian of Norwich (whose *Revelations of Divine Love* are grounded in the journey of the self in God).

Each year, the Bible Gateway website publishes a chart of the most searched-for Bible verses in the previous twelve months. The most popular verse is almost always John 3:16: 'For God so loved the world ...' However, the verse which is usually second is Jeremiah 29:11: '"For surely I know the plans I have for you", says the Lord, "plans for your welfare and not for harm".' It is not hard to see how this might be a turn to the self favourite. It speaks of a God who is interested in 'you' and has a plan for 'you'.[11] Even if some Christians are not finding resources for the self in their churches, the popularity of this verse suggests that many Christians are finding this support in their Bibles.

There are indeed churches which foster a heightened attention to the self. In Kendal, Heelas and Woodhead found congregations of 'experiential difference', congregations which had a conservative theology, but also paid attention to the experience of the individual. Most often, those were congregations from the evangelical-charismatic wing of the Church. In these churches, much of the worship and teaching was focused on God, and particularly the Spirit, 'within me' and courses were run to offer inner healing, support for parenting or development of one's own spiritual gifts.[12] It should be no surprise, given the turn to the self, and also their resistance to Disenchantment, that it is these kinds of churches which continue to experience the highest rates of growth in the United Kingdom.[13]

Blind Man

The recovery of the self, particularly where it has been neglected in the mainline, will be vital to its renewal. But will we be ready for the disturbance which will follow an influx of newly trans-formed true-selves?

At the beginning of John 9, we meet a former blind man who has been healed on the Sabbath. In the story, there is a sense that his sight is a symbol for his whole being – when his eyes have been healed, his whole person has also been healed.

When his neighbours try to deny that this is the same man they previously knew, he insists on being recognised, 'I am he, I am he', he keeps repeating. The religious authorities have no space in their rules for this kind of renewal. Under pressure, the man's parents distance themselves from their newly trans-formed son, but he is a resilient opponent. Repeatedly the Pharisees question him, but he will not deny his story, 'One thing I do know, that though I was blind, now I see,' he declares (John 9:25). He will not be cowed by the Pharisees and their aspersions; he knows what happened to him and, despite the Pharisees' pressure, he will not deny it. Not only does he value his new self, he also trusts it.

If we in the mainline are to become places where people become themselves, we will need to check our impulse to censor their stories of renewal for they will not fit within our regular categories. Recently a young woman, who had come to faith after, in her own words, previously seeking validation from academic success and boys, was baptised in our church. As part of the service, I asked her to give her testimony. I had planned that this would be an interview – I would ask questions and keep the conversation 'on track'. Beth had other ideas. Produc-ing a smartphone with the Notes application open, she began to read what was written before I could even ask my first ques-tion. This would be her script, not mine: and thus her story led into territory and conclusions about which I never would have asked, and was all the more powerful for having done so. This is very much at the soft end of the holy disturbance which will occur when, hopefully, newly redeemed selves find their home in our mainline churches. If we want to affirm identity, if we want to affirm the self, then we must be ready for our conventions to be broken.

Tamar

Married into the embryonic nation of Israel, Tamar, whose story is told in Genesis 38, was not given the best of men. Er, her first husband, was killed by the Lord on account of unspecified 'wickedness'. As was the custom, she married his brother Onan, who did not want any children if they were to be counted as his brother's, and so spilled 'his seed upon the ground'. This greatly displeased the Lord, and Onan too was put to death. Tamar's father-in-law Judah, now wary of losing his third son Shelah, sends Tamar back to her kin, explaining that Shelah is not yet of age. Within Judah's warped logic, Tamar is to be blamed for the sins of his sons.

As the years pass, Tamar perceives that no third marriage is coming her way. Does she quietly accept the obscurity that her father-in-law would prefer? Not at all. And why? Does she act out of duty to the memory of her dead husbands? Is she primarily motivated by a desire to provide her neglectful in-laws with an heir? Neither of these things. The only conclusion we can draw is that what Tamar does next, she does for herself.

Hearing that a recently widowed Judah is shortly to depart on a visit to his sheepshearers, Tamar hatches a plan. With an apparent inkling for her father-in-law's predilections, she covers her face in the manner of a prostitute and waits by the road on which Judah is due to pass. As she had anticipated, he approaches and asks to sleep with her. Tamar asks what he is willing to pay; he offers a goat kid, but since this is not to hand he gives over his personal ring, staff and cord by way of guarantee. And then, through her father-in-law, something happens for Tamar which had never occurred with either of her husbands: she conceives. Days later, Judah sends the promised goat via a friend, but 'the prostitute' is no longer to be found, and Judah resigns himself to losing his personal effects.

When, three months later, Judah is informed that his now pregnant daughter-in-law has been 'playing the whore', he erupts in rage and, assuming the role of righteous patriarch, demands Tamar be brought out and burned. As she is being brought out, doubtless surrounded by the shouts and taunts of the mob, she sends a message to her father-in-law, along with his ring, staff and cord: 'It was the owner of these who made me pregnant.' At this the truth is revealed to Judah. He now acknowledges that 'she is more in the right than I'. Tamar is spared and, in time, gives birth to twins, one for each brother (it could be said) who had failed in their duty towards her.

Tamar broke every one of my childhood commandments:

'Do not lie' – she concealed her true identity.
'Do not steal' – she held on to Judah's ring, staff and cord.
'Dirty' – she 'played the whore'.
'Selfish' – what Tamar did, she did for herself.

To powerful men around her, Tamar was cursed, a problem to be removed and an obligation to be evaded. She, for her part, could have internalised all that others thought of her and waited passively in her parents' house for the years to pass and eventually to die. Had Tamar chosen that path, we would never have known her name. Instead, with a striking sense that she was worthy of saving, she broke every societal convention, cared for herself, and thus her story became celebrated within the story of Israel (Ruth 4:12). And not only within Israel, for at the beginning of Matthew's Gospel we read these words: '... and Judah the father of Perez and Zerah by Tamar ...' (Matt. 1:3).

Tamar has a unique distinction. She is the first woman to be named in the entirety of the New Testament. Within the Christian story of salvation, the first woman to be named is an individual who deployed cunning and guile, who refused to accept male neglect, who broke the rules and, in doing so, carried the seed to the next generation. Part of being saved is to understand, even in desperate circumstances, the worth and importance of 'being me'.

Bringing Me to Church

The question remains: how might mainline churches be better places for our dying to the false-self, and embracing, in Christ, the true-self? There is much for mainline churches to learn from their charismatic sisters and brothers, none of it should be alien, all of it is Biblical: a stress on the life of the Spirit within, the telling of personal stories, the offering of support for healing and individual growth. And often, we may have to upset convention. Perhaps not by wrapping our faces in veils, and waiting for the passing of recently bereaved fathers-in-law, but there will be other means.

Twenty-five years ago I attended a night-time worship at the Greenbelt Arts Festival, organised by a group which included Graham, the mercurial genius to whom I will often refer in these pages. As a supremely gifted artist, Graham was driven by a conviction that if you thought long enough and pondered deeply enough, then the image you were looking for would emerge. This peculiar genius was to become evident on this particular evening.

The theme for worship was the same theme as our current chapter, the self. There were probably 300 of us in a large marquee – singing, reading, speaking and praying. I remember none of the details other than the moment, midway through worship, when each worshipper was given a parcel wrapped in paper with the description 'God's great gift to me'. What were these gift-wrapped squares? Each was 3 inches by 3 inches, solid and heavy. How could this gift possibly meet the exalted claim that had been made for it? As the service continued, the questions kept returning: 'What could this gift possibly be? God's great gift to me?' But, alas, we were given one strict instruction: 'no unwrapping until the end'.

Eventually we sang the last song, received the blessing, and opened our gifts; to our great shock, the gift did indeed meet its exalted billing, it did indeed show 'God's great gift to me'. What was it? A mirror. Each of us looked at ourselves. I looked at me. I have never forgotten the almost disbelieving joy of that moment. So much of me wanted to run away from it – this was too self-indulgent, or perhaps even heretical, but in that moment we were dared to receive the gift. Me in God. God's great gift to me *is* me.

And I think of an insight which Graham once had in relation to the story of the blind man in John 9. 'Think of that man as he walks to the pool,' said Graham. 'When he gets there, he crouches down, he cups his hands in the water and then starts to wipe the mud off his eyes; when the mud is gone, he dares to open them. He starts to take in what is in front of him; as he stares at the water he begins to make out a shape on its surface. What is the first thing he sees with his new eyes? ... The first thing he sees is his own reflection.' The first gift that Christ gives the former blind man is the ability to see himself. Because of Jesus, I can see me.

The renewal of the Church, and especially the mainline Church, does not begin with initiatives, or reorganisations, or strategies or plans. It begins in the rediscovery of a gospel which we have too often forgotten:

God is here.
Jesus saves.
And now, the Spirit is in me.
Leading to one further truth ...
I am loved. Yes, me.

6

Conservatives

Employed by one of the best-known fast-food chains in the United States, my sister-in-law occasionally organises international promotional events on her company's behalf. Needing a crowd of enthusiastic attendees for one such happening in Scotland in 2018, she reached out to a large independent Baptist church which was close to the event's location. I asked if I could accompany her when she went to meet the church's pastor, partly because I'd met him a number of years previously, but mainly because his church was now based in the former Church of Scotland building where my father had been minister.

Not having been inside the premises for twenty years, I was keen to see its current incarnation. In the 1960s, this place had been one of the great preaching stations of the Scottish Church. To attend evening services, queues would form on the street outside. By the 1980s, when our family were there, the crowds had gone but the congregation had a new mission: offering hospitality, prayer and support to those who worked and lived in the city centre. These included many who were homeless, or who struggled with addiction.

A sense of loss still lingered. Everywhere there were monuments to a 'glorious past': busts of distinguished former ministers; 'Standing-Room Only' signs from the 1960s were still kept in an upstairs cupboard, and a much smaller Sunday congregation worshipped within an enormous sanctuary. By the early 2000s, a few years after my dad's time there, merging with another congregation seemed the best option and the building was sold to the nearby independent Baptist church.

Many years later, tagging along with my sister-in-law, I noticed the feel of the place: it looked superb, a sophisticated blend of old and new. The pastor gave us a recent history of the congregation, including the fact that 'we now have 700 people at our morning services, and 300 in the evening'. Something visceral happened within me when I heard those numbers. I couldn't concentrate on anything else which was said; I just kept thinking about the '700 in the morning, 300 in the evening'. It was as if someone else's success had become my denomination's failure and, by some mysterious but irresistible extension, my own personal failure as well.

As the pastor continued, I recalled a conversation many years earlier with one of my housemates in Belfast. Rob was a youth worker with the Church of Ireland (part of the Anglican Communion). He had just taken his young people to an inter-church sports day, and it hadn't gone well. As he reflected on numerous defeats in various sports, Rob quietly stated an unavoidable truth: 'the Baptists won, the Baptists always win'. As I looked across the seats of my dad's old church, now filled by worshipping Baptists, I should have been glad that the kingdom of God was flourishing, but instead I could only hear Rob's voice in my head, quietly whispering: 'the Baptists won, the Baptists always win'.

The Names We Use

Before going further, it's important to say that this is not actually a chapter about Baptists. It's a chapter about a particular mainline experience: that of watching more conservative congregations prosper while we experience decline.

For our current purposes, the word 'conservative' relates to expressions of Protestant faith which emphasise the inspired (and often inerrant or infallible) authority of the whole Bible, and consequently a sharp discontinuity with contemporary cultural norms relating to, for example, human sexuality and female leadership. I will use the word 'liberal' to relate to expressions of Protestant faith which question or soften these positions and which also heighten the significance of reason or experience in our understanding of faith. Neither of these words is wholly satisfactory and they will only be used as shorthand when necessary. It's also important to note that every denomination and congregation appears more diverse the closer you become. There are many members of so-called conservative denominations who would hold views which may be described as liberal, and many mainliners who would hold views which may be described as conservative. Indeed, mainline denominations are not liberal denominations; instead, they are marked by their wide plurality and often refer to themselves as a 'broad church'.

A Changing Picture

Over the last fifty years, the pain of mainline loss has been compounded, if we are honest, by the growth of more conservative congregations. This growth has conformed to the 'Kelley Thesis' (named after Dean M. Kelley, the author of the 1972 book, *Why Conservative Churches Are Growing*), which attributes the growth of conservative churches to higher levels of congregational commitment, purpose and identity. Other commentators have suggested that during a disorienting period of cultural change, such congregations may offer a reassuring return to the certainties of the past.[1] However, others, including conservative leaders themselves, have argued that their growth is a result of theological faithfulness and that mainline decline is an inevitable result of doctrinal and moral infidelity. This is an argument which has troubled a great number of mainliners more than we might admit.

A high-level survey of the recent ecclesiastical landscape would appear to vindicate the 'Kelley Thesis'. Even within mainline denominations themselves, their more conservative congregations have often become their largest congregations (an interesting exception is the rise of Anglican and Episcopal cathedrals) and congregations with the largest numbers of young people have also tended to be conservative.[2]

However, a closer look reveals some important nuances. First, numerous North American scholars have pointed out that immigration rather than theology appears to be the more significant factor in much congregational growth. Also, it appears that it is the higher levels of commitment and identity engendered by a conservative theology, rather than the theology itself, which is a key factor. A huge survey of North American churches in 2010 found that both 'very conservative' and 'very liberal' congregations were growing, and that the most significant declines had been among those describing their theological stance as 'moderate'.[3] This increased sense of identity would also explain the growth of conservatism in other traditions such as Roman Catholicism.

The second important qualification to the 'Kelley Thesis' is a much more recent phenomenon: over the past two decades, many conservative churches have also begun to experience their own decline. Since 2015, in the United Kingdom, with the notable exception of some Diaspora, charismatic and smaller Reformed denominations, most conservative denominations and congregations have experienced a loss in attendance numbers.[4] In the United States in 2020, after many years of decline, the number of white evangelical Christians fell below those identifying as mainline;[5] and in 2022 the largest conservative denomination in the United States, the Southern Baptist Convention – which had been reducing in size since 2016 – lost almost half a million members.

How should mainline churches respond to this complex picture?

Sectarian

Mainline churches should continue to resist the suggestion made in some quarters that they should emulate the success of more conservative churches by becoming more 'sectarian'.[6] Not only is this advice becoming increasingly dated as conservative churches face their own experience of loss, but to become sectarian would conflict with an inherent element of mainline identity which is our diversity. How might this diversity become a positive, rather than a lukewarm tolerance?

The answer is that we must first embrace our diverse identity, and be less worried about the fortunes of other denominations. Think of that great saint of broad catholic identity, St Peter. Being Peter around the Beloved Disciple John cannot have been easy.[7] It was John who sat closest to Jesus at the Last Supper, John who stayed faithful during Jesus' last days, John who first reached the tomb on Easter Sunday ('the Beloved won, he always wins'), and John who first recognised Jesus on the shore of Lake Tiberias.

However, despite his repeated failures and apparent second-best-ness, Peter retains his calling. In his beautifully tender restoration, where the threefold affirmation of love echoes his earlier threefold denial, Peter is validated and called. His apparent inadequacy in relation to the Beloved Disciple is never mentioned: Peter is still to feed the sheep, tend the lambs and, in his last moments, to die a death which glorifies God. When Peter does notice the Beloved Disciple following him, one can sense his exasperation as he asks Jesus, 'What about him?' Jesus answers, 'If it is my will that he remain until I come', articulating yet another possibility where the Beloved might outdo Peter, 'what is that to you?' Jesus ends the conversation by repeating his earlier command to Peter, 'Follow me!' (John 21:22). The calling of the mainline is to follow Jesus, and not – to put it bluntly – to follow any other disciple, even one as Beloved as John.

Embracing Diversity

What, though, of the charge that the breadth and diversity of the mainline has been a factor in its demise? The charge that mainline congregations struggle to maintain a strong identity when their congregations contain such a diversity of influences, theological positions and preferred styles of worship? Here we might learn from the New Testament congregation of which we know the most with regard to its struggles with unity and diversity: the Church of Corinth.

The Corinthian struggles with difference are named in the

opening lines of 1 Corinthians. 'It has been reported to me ...
that there are quarrels among you,' says Paul (1:11). By naming
these so early, Paul is already acting counter to the common
mainline instinct that our divisions should be ignored for as
long as possible. We prefer our cans of worms unopened, and
our carpets underswept with all the troubling divides we would
rather avoid. But Paul continues. Having named the fact of
division, he then describes it: some, he says (perhaps the inclu-
sive radicals), are proudly claiming 'I am for Paul'. Others
(perhaps the institutional loyalists) are stating 'I am for Peter'.
Yet others (perhaps the studious intellectuals) are claiming 'I
am for Apollos'. Finally, there are those (whose divisiveness
hides behind a mask of piety) who simply claim 'I am for
Jesus'. Here, conflict is not described as a conflict of theology
(though doubtless such arguments raged) but a conflict of allegiance: allegiance to characters who, curiously, are off-stage.
How often is an issue of personal allegiance at the root of our
conflict, and very often it's allegiance to an individual who is
no longer here? How often is difference driven by allegiance
to a deceased parent, a charismatic teacher, a long-departed
minister, a formative youth worker, an international speaker
or a strong-minded friend? It seems that Paul is encouraging us
not only to name our conflicts, but also to detect the underlying
loyalties from which much of their energy derives.

At this point, it may be protested that sharply divided Corinth
is no window into the mainline: we may believe our churches
are very different from the Church in Corinth and that, for the
most part, they are cheerful oases of diversity and generally
happy families. But to this the following maxim may be offered:
'Beware the Church which quickly proclaims itself a happy
family.' In my experience this is almost always the rhetoric of
avoidance. Conflict and tensions lurk, often poisonously, but
are masked and suppressed by the practice of good manners.
Every church is home to tensions by virtue of being populated
by human beings. To name these tensions is not to paint ourselves as disputatious maniacs, but rather to admit that we are
the kind of community which the Church has always been.

Also, naming and describing our difference is a remarkably

potent move in ensuring that difference does not divide. I have frequently been surprised at the results of meetings and conversations where our differences are named. When facilitating, I have been terrified that matters were about to spiral out of control, only to discover later that the protagonists are enjoying friendly conversation in the car park after the meeting. This is, I believe, the first Corinthians lesson for the mainline: do not be vague about our breadth; rather, let us name and describe what it is.

Unity and Division

Paul's second response to Corinthian division is to ask a question: 'Has Christ been divided?' (1 Cor. 1:13). For him, our disputes do not only operate on a human level where they can become energy-consuming and destructive. Because they exist on a spiritual level, they also threaten something even worse: they attempt to tear at the very being of God. Every single member of the Corinthian Church is part of the body of Christ. There is a mystical one-ness between the Corinthians, simply because they are part of the Church. When attacking one another, they are attempting to tear at a spiritual reality; shockingly, according to Paul, they are attempting to dismember Jesus. The protagonists may envisage themselves engaged in a righteous war of purity, to rid the body of those who do not belong. But for Paul, regardless of the nature of the dispute it would seem, we are doing something wholly abominable. Any quarrel within the Church is, unknowingly, a desecration of the togetherness of Christ. It is spiritual violence.

One of the more tempting thoughts in any church dispute is to imagine that it would be better if one party were encouraged to leave, or be silenced, or be removed. This is the impulse to de-weed the field, to destroy with heavenly fire and to silence the unknown, each of which Jesus categorically rejects (Matt. 13:28; Mark 9:38; Luke 9:54). Jesus knows the violence of this. If there is rupture, then the violence of this reverberates in all who depart and in all who are left behind. We imagine that purity will cleanse us, but instead all are broken in the intensity of the purge.

This folly – that we would be pure if certain parties left – has bewitched the Church, siren-like, throughout its history. Schism always leads to disaster: whether it was Pope Innocent sanctioning the brutal Albigensian crusade against fellow Christians, so that wounds which did not respond to a poultice might be 'cut away with a knife';[8] the Scottish Disruption of 1843, a schism which I used to celebrate as the triumph of evangelical fervour, but which Liam Fraser has convincingly argued is one of the greatest causes of Secularisation in Scotland today;[9] or the Church splits of the 2010s during the human sexuality debates which left deep wounds in those who stayed and in those who left. Furthermore, speak to anyone who has suffered the trauma (and the word is not overused in this context) of being forced out of their congregation and one will hear of the ensuing years of hurt, and the never-resolved struggle to comprehend a senseless ordeal.

The desire to purge, to create purity, not only wounds the purged, but also instils an atmosphere of continued watchfulness and anxiety in those who stay. Sexual purity movements, for example, not only induce fear in those whose behaviour is deemed deviant, but also provoke paralysing anxiety within those who still adhere to their Church's teaching.[10] The lure of the pure is beguiling, but too often it wounds with injuries which take years to heal. The removal of any of the Corinthian parties is a thought which does not even occur to Paul. Quite the opposite. To purposefully perpetuate any congregational quarrel is unthinkable because it is, by definition, an assault on the very body of Christ.

The Word of the Cross

Paul's next response to the Corinthians' dispute seems surprising: he sets their divisions alongside 'the message about the cross' (1 Cor. 1:18). Here the cross is not referenced as a place of forgiveness between sinful humanity and a holy God (as Paul will expound in his letter to the Romans). Paul's primary perspective here is that the cross nullifies everything the world judges to be of importance: status, success, knowledge and power. Why is this understanding of the cross particularly pertinent in Corinth? At this point, we might benefit from understanding something of the city's background.

The Corinth to which Paul wrote had only recently been refounded by the Romans. It was a city of fresh opportunity. Perfectly sited for trade, the city was constantly drawing in merchants and tradespeople from West and East with their slaves and their gods. To the north, in staid Athens, the hierarchies of prestige which mattered so much in the ancient world were long settled. Not so in Corinth. Here, for the ambitious and industrious, for the jostlers and the hustlers, there was still much scope for social advancement. However, alongside social flux came social anxiety. If status could be gained, then it could also be lost; and so, constantly watchful as to their precarious position, the proud would strut, the wealthy would brag, and the educated would boast.

Despite Paul's determined attempts to forge a radically non-hierarchical congregation, this persistent and nagging anxiety with regard to status had leaked into the Corinthian Church. It is these status anxieties which, it would appear, lurk behind the Corinthian divisions and are the reason why Paul reminds the Corinthians that every system of human rank has been nullified by the cross.

Paul has understood that the Church's disputes have not been driven by a neutral discussion of ideas. What is giving these disputes their energy is a deep anxiety: about who is winning, about who is a success, about who is blessed. These bitter arguments have not been driven by the noble quest for truth, despite their pious pretensions, but by the jostling and bustling of human pride.

Similarly, within a diverse congregation, and mainline congregations can be very diverse, Paul's approach might encourage us to better diagnose the root cause of our differences, especially when these erupt into painful dispute. Too often our arguments are not born of a desire for truth, but a desire to win. And in the light of the cross, such desire is exposed as pure folly. Similarly, we should be extremely wary of any approach to congregational renewal which is grounded in the aspiration for success. Instead, we must recall the word of the cross which stands wholly counter to the 'wisdom of the world' (1 Cor. 1:20), and which cherishes that which is thought low, despised or even nothing.

The Garden and the Building

Paul's final response to the Corinthian arguments is his lengthiest (1 Cor. 3:1–23). Here he recasts himself and his alleged opponent Apollos not as heroes of opposing factions but as complementary teachers. Paul imagines the Church as a garden: he planted; Apollos watered. He imagines a building: Paul laid the foundations; Apollos continued the work. Different teachers are not opponents, but instead are those we need at different times. I once heard of a new Christian who turned up at a 'more liberal' church – what did the congregation do? They suggested this person might be better suited to a neighbouring evangelical church for five years. 'After five years,' the 'more liberal' church said, 'you may wish to come back to us.' I love the wisdom and the generosity of this – which sees different theological perspectives not as adversaries, but as participants in the same drama, appearing on stage during different seasons, but held by a common purpose and a common story. In the same spirit, we mainliners might note several lessons which could be profitably learned from our conservative sisters and brothers.

First, in conservative worship, whether Reformed or charismatic, there is often a marked attention to the presence of God. In Chapter 2, we argued that to seek God's presence is the key missional imperative of the mainline Church. When, for example, charismatic congregations worship, often for prolonged periods, they sense an intimacy which is not unlike the intimacy of Jesus and the Father in John's Gospel. In a disenchanted age, the conservative instinct, in both its Reformed and charismatic manifestations, to invoke the presence of God is probably their most important lesson to the mainline.

Second, as we have also noted, conservative churches, and particularly those described as evangelical-charismatic, are often good at attending to the self; to deploy an oft-repeated analogy from airline safety announcements, they are good at insisting their members have applied their own oxygen mask before proceeding to assist others.[11]

Third, conservative churches are often passionate evangelists. There used to be such a thing as ecumenical evangelism, or even liberal evangelism; evangelism was not the preserve of conservative congregations. In Scotland, George MacLeod, not usually regarded as conservative, was a passionate evangelist. During the early days of the ecumenical (and supposedly liberal) World Council of Churches, much attention was paid to evangelism. The 'Tell Scotland' movement of the 1950s (as we shall see later) harnessed the energies of local evangelists from across the theological spectrum; this is a dynamic which we need to recover.

Fourth, conservatives are very often enthusiasts. As we saw in Chapter 2, there is an intrinsic link between church growth and the enthusiasm of its members.[12] Enthusiasts attract non-members and subsequently create more enthusiasts. Mainliners must learn from the culture of entrepreneurial enthusiasm, so often found in conservative congregations.

Fifth, conservative churches are often great church planters. Less in thrall to traditional structures, they have a genius for discovering new forms of church life. In our Scottish context, it is the Free Church of Scotland which leads the way in planting churches. Over twenty years, it has developed approaches for finding new locations, training gifted leaders, and providing essential support. To learn how to plant new churches, we will need the wisdom of those in conservative denominations.

Sixth, conservative congregations often have a younger median age than mainline congregations. This is a much wider topic, but if it is correct that in the early years of faith we often require approaches to worship which inhabit contemporary genres of music, and theological accounts which espouse clarity alongside mystery, then both these require to be taken seriously by mainline congregations – without compromising their own diverse identity.

Finally, despite our arguments with the 'Kelley Thesis', it is probably correct to assert that conservative churches often engender higher levels of commitment from their members.[13] The German martyr Dietrich Bonhoeffer famously criticised the institutional churches of his day for their 'cheap grace ... grace without discipleship, grace without the cross, grace without Jesus Christ'. We are called to recover 'costly grace' which is 'the treasure hidden within a field ... the pearl of great price to buy which the merchant will sell all that he has'.[14] Too often mainline churches have asked too little, received too little, and given too little. Their economies of grace and discipleship have become too shrunken. By contrast, Paul ends his discussion of the Corinthians' disputes with one of the most profound, universal and generous affirmations of any of his letters. To those terrified of being left behind in a perpetually competitive culture, to those who have forgotten the value they give to and derive from one another, to those whose economy of grace has become too reduced, he affirms:

> For all things are yours, whether Paul or Apollos or Cephas or the world or life or death or the present or the future – all belong to you, and you belong to Christ, and Christ belongs to God. (1 Cor. 3:21–23)

By facing dispute honestly, Paul has led the Corinthians, and us, to the deepest truths: that we belong to one another, that we belong to God; and to the deepest belonging of all, that which lies within the very being of the divine: 'Christ belongs to God.'

For me, the most powerful lessons about our fundamental unity came when I lived in Belfast. In Northern Ireland, from the early 1970s until the late 1990s, centuries-old tensions had erupted into the horrendous violence of 'the Troubles'. Ken Newell, a Presbyterian minister, alongside Gerry Reynolds, a Catholic priest, were part of a small group of clergy who actively worked to bring about reconciliation. This was difficult, draining and often dispiriting work. Ken and Gerry, often in secret, would meet with politicians and even terrorists, trying to understand concerns, identify common ground, and imagine what compromises might reduce tension and lead to peace.

I do not know what was said of Father Gerry within the Catholic Church, but I do know that Ken Newell was regarded as a liberal traitor by many in his own denomination and community. Though wounded by attacks on his faith and integrity, and too often threatened, he would unrelentingly pursue any avenue which might lead to peace. Naturally warm and gregarious, he would become fierce when confronting apathy or hypocrisy: whether that was corralling fellow Protestant clergy to attend the funeral of a murdered Catholic, or confronting the falsehoods of politicians, regardless of whether they were Unionist or Republican. For both Ken and Gerry, their peace-making was belligerently determined, full of risk, and very often it seemed – especially during the 1980s and early 1990s – without the possibility of success.

In the early 2000s, I was the youth worker in Ken's congregation in Belfast, Fitzroy Presbyterian. At this point, the Good Friday Agreement of 1998 had ushered in the possibility of peace, but there was still much to be done. Ken and Gerry continued the work of peace-making, undergirded, as always, by their great friendship. When not celebrating Mass in his own parish, Father Gerry would often attend our services, including one particular all-age service in 2001.

All-age services had had a vexed history in our congregation and everybody dreaded them: adults found them banal, children were rarely engaged, and with dozens of unfocused ideas they often lasted an age. Chastened by previous liturgical disasters, I had worked hard to put together the perfect all-age liturgy: energetic, fun, insightful, and held together by a non-negotiable timetable. This service would not drag: the benediction would be pronounced at 11:50am precisely!

Up until 11:40am we were doing splendidly. Then at 11:41am it seemed that God spoke to Father Gerry who, during the next song, moved out of his pew and began walking towards the front of the church. Even as Gerry walked, I had a sense of what might be about to happen: Gerry would want to speak and my schedule would be ruined. He may have been a living saint and hero of the peace process, but at this precise moment (now 11:43) I was furious with him.

'Neil, I'd like to say a few words, if that would be okay,' he asked. How could I say no? This was Father Gerry. 'Okay, Father,' I muttered, hoping he would pick up on my reluctance.

Gerry moved to the lectern, and began to speak ...

'I've been thinking,' he announced in his thick Limerick accent.

'I've been thinking,' he repeated (again!).

'I've been thinking about the Trinity.'

'Oh no!' I thought. 'This is a disaster, abstract theological speculation in the middle of an all-age worship which needs to finish in six minutes' time.'

'I've been thinking about the Trinity, and how it is that the Father is the Father for the Son, and the Son is the Son for the Father, and the ...'

'He's going to go round the whole of the Trinity!' I inwardly protested. 'Hurry up, Gerry, get going, we get the point!'

'... and the Son is the Son for the Spirit, and the Spirit is the Spirit for the Son, and the ...'

We were not going to finish in five minutes.

'... and the Spirit is the Spirit for the Father, and the Father is the Father for the Spirit.

'And I've been thinking, that the one is different from the other, for the sake of the other. Their difference is the gift they offer to each other.

'And I, who am Catholic, am Catholic for you, you who are Protestant.

'And you who are Protestant are Protestant for me, me who is Catholic.

'The difference we are to one another is the gift we give to one another.

'And this is rooted in the very being of God.'

I cannot remember any other thing about that service. I can only remember what Father Gerry had said: that the difference we are to one another is a gift we give to one another, and this is rooted in the very being of God. This was not taught as an abstract philosophical truth but spoken in a city which had been torn apart by violence, and by a priest who had given his life for the cause of peace. When receiving the International Pax Christi award in 1999, Father Gerry Reynolds said these words:

> We are learning that the destiny of Christians in Northern Ireland is to help make an end of the Reformation conflict. We discover that those we used to call 'outsiders' are truly 'brothers and sisters' in Christ and that we hold our traditions not against but for one another. We are learning that 'Love one another as I have loved you' is a call to us not only as individual persons, but also as congregations and communities of the church ... it has been said that 'divided churches cost lives'.[15]

In Protestant mainline churches our diversity may have cost us growth, but to give it up would cost us even more – it would cost us our very selves. And when faithfully discerned, we will continue to discover that our diversity is not a burden, but a gift, leading us into the very being of God.

7

Middle

Over the last thirty years, the most painful mainline experience of diversity has related to questions of human sexuality, and of trying to find a middle path between apparently irreconcilable views. This is my own experience of trying to find that middle path, a version of middle which eventually caused me to go deep as well as wide, and which taught me a similar truth to that discovered by Ken Newell and Gerry Reynolds in Northern Ireland: that our mainline diversity is not a threat to our existence, but instead an essential part of who we are.

Before continuing, I want to give suitable warning that this chapter goes back into some painful and contentious moments. I have sought to be as faithful as possible to the different viewpoints described, as well as the truth of my own story. However, I am painfully aware that there will be points where I haven't managed to achieve this and, for such moments, I apologise in advance and also promise to keep listening, to embody the committed 'middle' which this chapter is about.

The Early Story

When coming to faith in my late teens, my views on sexuality became distressingly more complicated. Previously I had believed that, without question, there was no moral difference between being gay and being straight. However, within evangelicalism, with which I now identified, we were often warned not to 'pick and choose' from the scriptures. If one believed that 'God is love' (1 John 4:16) and that Jesus came to preach the Good News to the poor (Luke 4:18), then it was also imperative to believe that for a man to lie with a man was an 'abomination' (Lev. 18:22). Any form of sexual expression outside of marriage was a harmful departure from the pattern of creation, and any vacillation on this issue was to risk one's own salvation (1 Cor. 6:9).

Four years in Northern Ireland had introduced me to dialogue between Protestant and Catholic, and the discovery that pragmatic, complicated compromises were not just good – but also saved lives. But on the issue of human sexuality, no similar resolution seemed possible. I oscillated between traditionalist and revisionist views: there were periods when I instinctively felt that the inclusion of lesbian and gay Christians was akin to the abolition of slavery, or the ordination of women – an issue on which the Church would, in time, have to move. But in other moments I could not escape the consistency of the scriptures. As one of my ministers put it on this issue, in the Bible there was 'no melting of the ice'.

Within the Church of Scotland, my introduction to this debate came in 2006, when asked to sit on a presbytery committee, formed to examine proposals for the blessing of civil partnerships.[1] Tasked with the group's Biblical research, I plunged myself into an analysis of Romans 1, and the etymological origins of the Leviticus word 'abomination'. When I produced a summary table which was the very model of even-handedness, the committee were delighted. With the exception of one elder who thought the whole debate a nonsense: gay people loved each other, and God is love.

Through that research, however, I was beginning to harden, increasingly convinced by the argument that 'gender complementarity', the innate compatibility of male and female relationships (and, by extension, the non-compatibility of same-gender relationships), was baked into the order of creation. A scholar called Robert Gagnon had put this traditionalist argument forward with such apparently irrefutable logic that little room was left for doubt. I could no longer sit in the middle. Reluctantly, I conceded that Gagnon was almost certainly right.[2]

Only later would I read the words of a Catholic scholar, James Alison, concerning unassailable arguments. Admitting

﹍ call to live out creation sexuality is 'a task which is
arduous but possible',[3] Alison then added that 'this is a watertight argument and the moment an argument is watertight ...
it is likely to be an argument born from resentment, not from
grace'. Watertight arguments may lure us with their certainty
and their elimination of troubling unknowns; but these can
also be airless places, different in character, perhaps, from the
vitality of the gospel.

A Divided Denomination?

In 2009, discussion in the Church of Scotland became considerably more intense with the proposed induction of a gay
minister, Scott Rennie, to a congregation in Aberdeen. After
much debate, this was allowed by our General Assembly, but a
temporary moratorium was placed upon any similar appoint-
ments. There followed a series of reports, stated trajectories
and debates until, by 2013, it was clear that some kind of resolution was required.

A Theological Commission had proposed two possibilities:
'option 2a' affirmed same-sex relationships while 'option 2b'
reaffirmed a traditionalist stance.[4] In the lead-up to that year's
Assembly, there was much campaigning and organising. A new
generation of evangelical leaders concluded that, at previous
Assemblies, evangelicals had been insufficiently organised.
I confess that I found some of these emerging leaders a little
difficult to be around but, as with Robert Gagnon, had to con-
cede that they were probably right. They projected a certainty
which was difficult to resist, and a steely focus on their end
goal: winning the vote.[5]

During the Assembly's debate, the previous year's moderator,
who was regarded as an evangelical, proposed a compromise
motion which would eventually break the impasse of the previous ten years. However, I was not yet ready to move to his
middle ground. I could find no way past Gagnon and his unassailable arguments. Citing my understanding of Jesus as one

who welcomed all while retaining a traditional ethical view, I spoke in favour of 'option 2b', the traditionalist motion.

What I didn't realise at the time was the effect this speech had had on my gay friends. For them, these were not mere words at an increasingly irrelevant church gathering. Rather, it felt like yet another betrayal, yet another moment when the Church, albeit in refined and gentler language, was refusing to welcome the person they were. One said it 'was like a kick in the stomach'. Another friend, who at the time I didn't even know was gay, such was her concern to protect herself from the judgement of Christian friends, had screamed 'Nooooo!' as she watched online. My friend Graham, a long-time ally of lesbian and gay people, said that the person speaking at the Assembly didn't sound like me. I don't know how he'd spotted this internal dissonance, but he was right. For when I'd been making my speech, there had been another voice in my head, refusing to be silenced, saying, 'Neil, do you really believe this to be true?'

On the train home to Glasgow that night, I found myself with four people who are also some of my heroes: Molly and John Harvey, and Mary and John Miller. These four have, over many years, lived lives of radical Christian commitment. They too had been attending the debate and were hugely disappointed at the outcome, but for different reasons. For them, the agreed compromise had not gone nearly far enough: the call of the Church was to affirm, without question, all loving relationships, gay or straight. For John and Mary, contact with Christians in a place that I would afterwards remember as Croatia[6] had demonstrated to them, all too clearly, the need for unequivocal affirmation of gay and lesbian relationships. If the Church continued to reiterate its traditional condemnation of same-sex relationships, prejudice would be legitimised and, inevitably, be amplified into homophobic violence. Mary, in particular, did not hold back on her opinions about my General Assembly speech: 'What on earth were you doing in there?' she asked. It was an uncomfortable journey back to Glasgow.

A Series of Events

Next day at the Assembly, I found myself talking to a woman called Pam Skrgatic, one of the volunteers in the Assembly's cloakroom. Pam's son Paul, who I knew was gay, had been at school with me.

'How's Paul doing?' I asked.

'Wonderful,' she exclaimed, 'he and Michael got married two weeks ago. It was just the most fantastic occasion, just amazing!' Pam beamed. I beamed with her. In my spirit I was delighted for her and for Paul, inwardly joyful in a way that I hadn't experienced when arguing for 'option 2b'. What was going on? The logic and the learning said '2b', but in my spirit something else was stirring. The following morning, I prayed. Literally on my knees, I asked God to give me a word and, to my great shock, a word came, saying 'Paul Skrgatic is from Croatia'. This was totally unexpected.

I began to question myself. Was I dredging up some long-forgotten memory, and attributing this to God? Although I had a distant recollection that Paul was from Yugoslavia (as it had been when we were at school), this was not something I'd thought about for years, certainly not in the past few days. I was trying desperately to tell myself that this had been auto-suggestion, rather than divine word. Surely God wouldn't say such a specific thing, nor something that was bound to lead me down a revisionist path? But 'Paul Skrgatic is from Croatia' tied my experience on the Monday – Mary and John Miller's outrage at homophobic violence – to my experience on the Tuesday: happiness that Paul and his partner had got married.

Two weeks later I was still troubled and realised there was only one way to check this. I texted Paul. The conversation is still on my phone ...

'Paul, it was really good to bump into your Mum at this year's General Assembly, where she looks after us so well, and she was saying that you are doing well. Complete random question: where is the name Skrgatic from? I remember you once talking about it but couldn't remember. Anyway, apologies for being random, hope you are doing well, Neil.'

Paul replied:

'Hi Neil. Good to hear from you. Skrgatic is Croatian as my dad is from Zagreb.'

I felt like a sinking ship, holed below the waterline. Paul is actually from *Croatia*. What is God playing at? I might have persisted in my uneasiness, hoping it would eventually subside, but Graham had other ideas. He contacted me to say that the poet Pádraig Ó Tuama was leading a workshop on the Church's welcome of lesbian and gay Christians: 'He's coming to Langside, Neil, you should go and listen to him.' I wasn't eager to go but Graham, with that persistent genius of his, kept reminding me, and so – not particularly enthusiastically – I went.

At this point, I actually thought I had either read or heard every argument in the 'lesbian and gay debate'. But there was something about the evening, the things Pádraig said and the way he said them; he had a wisdom which had grown from his many years as a gay man within the Catholic Church and also from working with conservative Christians in Northern Ireland. I remember his unwillingness to accept a stance where gay people were welcomed, but their relationships were not: 'How would you feel if you turned up at church and, as a condition of membership, they asked you to leave your wife?' he asked. For Pádraig, the person you love is not a removable part of your identity and this is no different if the person you love is of the same gender. To him, love was a calling to be true to the deepest parts of yourself; it was not something to be suppressed or removed. There was something else about Pádraig: he shone. There was a wisdom, a beauty and a poise to him. It was very difficult to deny that the Spirit might be in that encounter – and also in him.

Re-reading the Scriptures

I was failing to get rid of my highly inconvenient 'Croatia moment'. My last defence was the scriptures. I had done the work; I had written well-balanced reports: the arguments were watertight. But here too I was to become undone. I had already begun to question the kind of relationships which Paul describes in Romans 1. These did not look like the loving, committed relationships of many of my gay friends. But the story which changed me was the story of Peter's vision and the Church's inclusion of the Gentiles in chapters 10–11 of Acts.

This episode begins when Peter is praying: he enters an ecstatic trance ('ecstatic' literally means 'moved out of place' which is a good picture of all that was about to happen); he sees a sheet containing every four-footed creature, including those which the scriptures tell him are unclean. 'Get up, kill and eat,' a voice instructs him. Peter protests, but the voice repeats itself twice more. Through some divinely orchestrated encounters, Peter then finds himself at the house of a Roman centurion called Cornelius. Cornelius and his companions are of course 'unclean' Gentiles. But it is here, while Peter is recounting his vision of the animals and declaring that 'God shows no partiality' (Acts 10:34–35), that the Holy Spirit falls on all who are listening: Gentile and Jew. Thus, through a combination of visions, divine words, serendipitous encounters and the undeniability of the Spirit's presence within those previously considered beyond the bounds of salvation, Peter's map of insiders and outsiders is radically changed.

At no point does this story mention sexuality, let alone same-sex sexuality. And yet it is this episode, almost more than any other, which seems to have led traditionalists like me to affirm the relationships of LGBTQ+ Christians.[7] There are so many resonances: the moment of being taken out of place; the voice which questions Peter's watertight tradition and his vehement desire to defend it; the 'coincidence' of unexpected encounters; and the power of seeing the Holy Spirit's presence in those previously considered outsiders. In this story, the full inclusion of outsiders is grounded upon faith in Christ but not on their wholesale acceptance of Peter's worldview, and while they are converted Peter must also change.

With respect to the Church of Scotland's ongoing discussions, I had kept my evolving thoughts private, but in early 2014 I was contacted by a local journalist. The Scottish Parliament had just passed the 'Marriage and Civil Partnership Bill' which legalised same-sex marriage. Asked to comment, I did not wish to sound equivocal in any way (I was remembering Mary Miller) and so I welcomed the passing of the Act and the 'inclusion of all in our society, regardless of sexuality'.

'Local minister goes against Church's own teaching on gay marriage', read the following week's headline. My own congregation was divided: some applauded; others were shocked. One of my ministerial colleagues, a good friend, was appalled at the damage done. When the article was posted on a national website, I received calls from further afield. This is a fraction of what gay people experience when they come out, but it was still a level of publicity and scrutiny which I desperately wanted to disappear.

As I had been at the General Assembly, so too on this occasion I was taken aback by the strength of response from my gay friends: Pádraig said he was surprised and was remarkably affirming; Alex who had shouted 'Noooo!' at her computer screen during the Assembly said she had wept with gratitude while reading the article. Christian friends reacted in different ways: a minister who had previously led evangelicals in their opposition to same-sex marriage told me that he too had recently changed his mind. Other very good friends, often over many coffees, said they continued to wrestle with the subject, but remained convinced that the traditionalist view was the unarguable teaching of scripture.

Perhaps the most surprising response came from an older friend and mentor who told me that during the early 2000s, while working for a Christian organisation which had been part of the 'Keep the Clause' campaign, a group of Christians had visited his office to pick up some campaign literature (Clause 28, or section 2A as it was in Scotland, prohibited schools from promoting or normalising same-sex relationships). This group had time for coffee and conversation, during which, my friend says, he was 'in no doubt that I was meeting with born-again, Holy Spirit-filled Christians'. At the end of the conversation, one of their number said to him, 'I need to tell you who we are: all of us are gay', and added that they all belonged to a congregation which affirmed same-gender relationships. They were wholly opposed to 'the clause'. My friend was stunned. 'You could have knocked me over with a pin,' he now recalls.

A Better Kind of Middle

With my own congregation being, like most other mainline congregations, a mix of traditionalists, revisionists and those not sure, we resolved to have an evening where we would listen to one another's views. The intention was not that we seek to change one another's minds, but rather that we would try to better understand the place where each of us stood. Three other ministers would join us: one to facilitate, the other two to tell their own story of being traditionalist or revisionist. After each one had spoken, members of the congregation began to share their own perspectives.

Almost everybody in the meeting spoke that night, but the contribution which I most remember came from a surprising source: a couple called George and Ishbel. Warm and hospitable, with a preference for the formal, George and Ishbel were stalwarts of our congregation: running stalls at the Christmas and summer fairs, bringing items they'd baked to coffee mornings, serving in the kitchen at church meals. Ishbel and her sister oversaw the flower rota and, unless they were on holiday, George and Ishbel never missed a Sunday. George much preferred it when I led services in robes and lamented that I rarely preached from the pulpit. Ishbel probably thought the same, but gently scolded him for being too outspoken. They were not the kind of people given to personal testimony. Theirs was a faith which you didn't readily speak about; instead, you showed it by the way you lived.

That evening, my recollection is that George and Ishbel had

arrived uncharacteristically late. Perhaps they had been anxious about coming along. For the early part of the evening, they sat quietly, listening to what others had to say. However, about two-thirds of the way through, Ishbel said, 'I would like to say something.' She was clearly nervous and produced some handwritten notes; laying them on her lap, she began to speak. George sat next to her, holding her hand. 'This is a story I have not told before, but I have permission to tell it,' she said.

Ishbel and George then told the story of their daughter Thora, who had discovered many years previously that she was gay. They spoke of their great hurt when, in their previous congregation, she had been asked to step down as a Sunday school teacher when this had become known. They also spoke of their great love for Thora's partner Tess, and their unequivocal support for them as a couple. Their reasoning was simple: 'How could it be wrong for two people to love each other?'

My strongest memory from that night was what happened at the end of the conversation. After closing remarks from our facilitator, almost everybody rose from their seats and gathered round Ishbel and George, hugging them in what eventually became a large collective embrace. This was even more remarkable because George and Ishbel were not 'huggy' people. But here we all were: traditionalist and revisionist, all together. At that point the labels mattered little. What counted was that George and Ishbel were family and we wanted to show it. We didn't all agree: I still don't know to what extent anyone changed their views that evening, but none of us could have been unchanged. And we discovered something deep in our souls: that which held us was far more important than that which threatened to split us apart.

I have often heard people say that 'we are a broad Church' or 'that which unites us is bigger than that which unties us'. These often feel like platitudes, a slightly flavourless desire that we stick together because falling out is just a little bit too unpleasant. The embrace around George and Ishbel that night was more than that; it was a profound moment of mutual belonging. It was a true picture of just how much our one-ness matters, when we realised that we were no longer quite so afraid of those in the congregation who held a different view. This was a middle-ness which knew itself, and also knew the breadth of love.

As we have already noted, studies suggest that a significant cause of mainline decline is our theological breadth. Churches which do not espouse a definite position, which are 'moderate' rather than 'very conservative' or 'very liberal', have been more likely to experience decline. And yes, sometimes that breadth tempts us to become bland or even voiceless. The invitation of the gospel is to go beneath our generalities, and discover a deeper, truer, more radical belonging. Through this, it might be that diversity itself would become one of our 'strong and defining' characteristics, one which becomes an essential part of our evangelism and also leads us more deeply into the very being of God.[8]

A decade after the 2013 General Assembly, the Church of Scotland remains a denomination which sits in the middle. Around the world, other mainline denominations, though at different points in their own debates, remain similarly diverse. Evangelicals have often stayed traditionalist; revisionists have continued to affirm. What kind of middle is this? Is it a begrudging accommodation, or might it be a calling? And is it a static agreement, or a commitment to move together? If, as has been argued, the hunger of the secular age is for an encounter with God, then might this diverse one-ness also lead us to holy ground, into that diverse one-ness which is of the very essence of God?

That word 'one' can be too easily passed over. Might it be for us that rapturous sense of 'one', of which Ephesians sings, 'one body, one Spirit ... one hope to which you were called ... one Lord, one Faith, one baptism, one God and Father of all who is over all and through all and in all'?

8

Structures

This is a chapter on a greatly underloved world: that of religious structures. This is the world which Jesus lambasted in his attacks on the temple and religious authorities, which the apostles escaped in the dynamic early days of the Church; and which, we are often convinced, has stifled the life of the mainline Church.

The world of structures is the world of committees, buildings, presbyteries, dioceses and councils; and of reports, policies and audits. More profoundly, a structure is also the set of behaviours, values and cultures which define our institutional world. This, surely, is a world which merits only cursory attention. Surely our renewal will spring from more inspiring places?

For we know, often from bitter experience, that work in this area has yielded little fruit. Many have concluded that the rebirth of the mainline Church will arrive when at last we free ourselves from the thickets of institutional inertia and return to the simplicity of the early Church or, if this is not possible, to the relative simplicity of more congregationally focused denominations.

But this disdain for structure is, I believe, a huge part of the problem. In this chapter we shall examine why we relegated the world of structure into becoming this unappreciated and undervalued realm, and why many of our attempts to address it have failed. We will also identify practices and ideas which may enable us to rediscover, without embarrassment, the joy and potency of this kind of work; practices and ideas which, far from diverting us from our core concerns, will draw us back into the very heart of our faith.

Naming the Powers

Though committees and governance are rarely mentioned in the New Testament, there is another frequently occurring word which has much to say in this arena: power. It is this concept, alongside related words such as ruler, authority and even throne, which might help us reclaim the importance of the structural world, and also show us how we might engage with it far more effectively.

The scholar and activist Walter Wink,[1] renowned for his work in this area, noted that whenever the New Testament refers to a ruler, authority or power this may be a reference to:

1 A visible institution or individual (e.g. Roman Empire).
2 A named ruler (e.g. Pontius Pilate).
3 An invisible spiritual power (e.g. a heavenly angel).
4 All of the above ('thrones or dominions or rulers or powers').

This led Wink to two key insights:

1 The language of power is prevalent throughout the New Testament. Powers matter.
2 A power is material and spiritual. It is a unified entity consisting of outer manifestations and an inner spiritual essence.

Both these insights will be essential in revitalising our structural work.

The Power of Powers

During the nineteenth century, numerous wealthy individuals and well-intentioned charities sought to improve the lives of the poorest people in Glasgow; these attempts nearly always failed because they lacked the scope and durability to bring about long-term change. Furthermore, through bypassing democratic representation, they aligned themselves with the prejudices of the elite, seeing the city's poorest people as, in essence, a problem to be contained or removed. Those participating in these initiatives did not usually comprehend that the very structures which enabled the wealthy to be so 'generous' were the exact same structures which ensured the poorest people remained poor.

By contrast, the most widespread and long-lasting reforms during this period came from a much-maligned institution: the city's council. It was the council, or the 'City Fathers' as they were referred to back then, which was responsible for the introduction of clean water, libraries, parks, transport, laundries, hospitals and refuse collection.[2] Structures – and in this case democratic structures – have considerable power.

As our secular age has turned to the individual self, we have forgotten the importance of structural power. There is only a limited amount that any one person can achieve on their own. We need structures to connect our efforts, hone our ideas, collect our talents, and focus these on a common goal. If this common effort is to be widespread, long-lasting and accountable, then it will require institutional structures in which to be held. Similarly, our aspirations to be free, hospitable or just will be mere talk unless we also form structures which make these values real. Structures matter. Powers matter,[3] which is why they were created by Christ at the beginning of the world (Col. 1:16).

One principal reason our structures cause us such pain is precisely because we give them such reluctant consideration. We joke that 'God so loved the world that he didn't send a committee', or yearn to be like independent congregations whose modus operandi is 'committee-lite', or criticise a focus on 'buildings rather than mission' as if these were two separate things. When treated this way, structures become like unloved children who must scream for attention; when this attention is given resentfully or thoughtlessly, or only with a desire to get on to something more important, then the cry grows louder, and we are unable to leave them alone. We need a better way of valuing our structural work.

Structures During Decline

Our already strong disdain for structure has become even more heightened in a context of decline. First, because our structural work simply hasn't delivered the renewal for which we hoped. How many mainliners have wrestled for years in committees, only to see their labours dismissed by a negative vote or, if enacted, still failing to bring about lasting change.

When our structural work fails to deliver, not only do we become disillusioned, but a second, darker mechanism becomes more prominent scapegoating. When recently attending a meeting of closure-threatened congregations, I was shocked that by far the loudest round of applause was given to the speaker who furiously argued that 'we shouldn't be shutting down congregations, we should be shutting down 121' ('121' being Church of Scotland shorthand for its central offices at 121 George Street in Edinburgh). Mainline denominations have rarely had easy relationships with their national headquarters, but in the context of decline these have come under increasing strain.[4] This is partly a result of the changing nature of headquarters work which in recent years has become more regulatory and support-based, work which by its very nature is confidential and not visible or appreciated by most church members. Additionally, it is centrally based staff who are often the messengers for difficult decisions. Therefore, in a context of pain, our national offices have become a relatively easy target. But if not national offices, then we will alight upon our presbytery or diocese, or perhaps our regional leaders (who have failed to give support), our clergy (who have failed to fill our pews), our youth workers (who have failed to produce enough young people) or our elders (who are supposedly resistant to change). The merit of these accusations is not the principal issue; rather, it is that we are in such pain that we need someone else to bear it.

This ancient practice of scapegoating frequently reappears in our structural work – surprisingly so since we allegedly live in a more enlightened age. Scapegoating is a mechanism which works by giving us an outlet for our frustrations and, if the expulsion is enacted, a temporary release from our pain. It is, though, ultimately futile; for, after a while, the powers begin to do their work, the old patterns re-emerge, and so too does our ache. Before long, we have need of another victim and the cycle begins again. The damage done to scapegoating's victims is immense, but so too is the damage done to the perpetrators, for they bear the guilt of the expulsion, and the anxiety of living in a system in which they may be next.

Valuing Structures in a Declining Institution

If it is the case that our already low regard for structure has become intensified in an era of decline, how do we find a better way? How do we value our structures and ensure our structural relationships heal? If, as we have already affirmed, we need structures for our work to have long-lasting and widespread effect, then how do we work towards healthy structures which will play their part in our overall renewal?

First, we must undo our primal instinct for scapegoating. This cannot be achieved through a general diktat that scape-goating be eliminated but requires profound spiritual work. Put in the starkest terms, scapegoating occurs when we feel the pain of our decline and become haunted by the fear that this has been our fault.

We need a better way of eliminating our sense of inadequacy or, to put it in even starker language, our sense of sin. The good news is that this lies at the very heart of the Christian gospel. Our calling is not to find the individual who is most responsible for failure and heap all blame upon her or him, but to recog-nise that our failure is partly our own and partly shared. This can be partly related to failures which long predated our own participation in the life of the Church, and can be partly related to changes in the wider society of which we have little con-trol. And we will never precisely untangle this whole mess of mistaken behaviour. We can keep trying to identify a principal culprit, or we can, in the words of John the Baptist, 'Behold the lamb of God who takes away the sin of the world' (John 1:36, ESV). The sin of the world includes the historic sins of the Church, the sins of 121, the sins of presbytery, the sins of the last minister, the sins of the bishop, the sins of me. He, the sacrificial lamb in John's language, takes the guilt of all of it away and offers us a new way to be human.

Mistakes will need to be addressed and lessons learned (more on this shortly) but the frenzied primal need for a sacrificial victim has been profoundly dismantled by the death and rising of Christ. Believing in this is deep spiritual work: it will involve scripture, prayer and confession. Embrace of the Eucharist, or Communion, is also central in recovering this profound sense of absolution. Not for the first time will we discover that redeeming our structural work brings us into the heart of our faith.[5]

Community

But though we may admit that much of our frustration with structures is misplaced, there still remain many areas of what can only be described as structural stupidity or, even worse, structural injustice. To engage here, we need to recall that the Church is always a community. Every committee is a community. So is every team, task group or panel.

First, this enables us to be honest concerning our own structural mistakes. To address the beam in our own eyes before attending to the speck in anyone else's (Matt. 7:1–5). Once we remember ourselves to be a Christ-held community, then belonging is assured and we have a far safer place in which to address the aspects of our work which are destructive, naïve, incompetent or unfair. We can admit our failures, be honest about our disagreements, and learn together.

Then we must recall that if every committee, task group or panel is a community, then so too is every other committee, task group or panel. When we stop seeing our structural landscape as a war of competing agencies, and instead as a network of Christ-held communities, then we can begin to address the not-infrequent moments in our structural life when we have difficulties with other bodies. At that gathering of congregations in which a speaker had urged us to 'shut down 121', it was remarkable how quickly the meeting's anger dissipated when it was pointed out that the people of '121' had themselves experienced severe cuts and now occupied only half the number of floors in their original building. This was a moment when we saw ourselves not as competing bodies, but as two communities sharing in the same experience. In remembering that we are fellow communities, we can better untangle our conflicts, discover what is ungrounded, and reconcile whatever issue has set us at odds. True community creates an atmosphere of grace where our problems become less frightening and infinitely more fixable.

In remembering that every committee is a community, we are also reminded that a principal part of a committee's life is simply to look after its people. A committee does have a key piece of work to achieve (we shall come to this in Chapter 11), but a key part of its life is simply to 'rejoice with those who rejoice' and 'weep with those who weep' (Rom. 12:15). When we face the cold secular winds of decline, we are called to inhabit that beautiful Irish proverb 'It is in the shelter of each other that we live'.

The key leadership thinker Ronald Heifetz (he of adaptive change) has said that this time of change requires 'structures that hold people together through the very conflictive, passionate, and sometimes awful process of addressing questions for which there aren't easy answers'. Margaret Wheatley, famous for her insight that in the current era we do not need heroes but hosts, has said that 'the primary way to prepare for the unknown is to attend to the quality of our relationships'.[6] Profound change requires strong community.

Making Strategy Sacred Again

Powers are also, as Walter Wink discovered, spiritual and material. We have forgotten that they are both. Recently I was in conversation with an individual who was utterly frustrated with a particular part of our denominational structures: the poor behaviour of partners and management; the inertia of committees; and the exhausting difficulty of attempting new ideas. What struck me about this conversation was that it was almost identical to a conversation I had had with another individual, in a similar role, ten years earlier. Over the subsequent decade, every single person in the organisation had changed, committees had been reorganised, attempts had been made at cultural change – and yet the fundamental issues had remained almost exactly the same. Why? Because every structure is the visible manifestation of an invisible internal spirit, a spirit which in this case had remained stubbornly unchanged.

Since powers are both material *and* spiritual, they must be engaged with both materially *and* spiritually. Walter Wink noted that 'liberals' tended to downplay the spiritual dimension, interpreting this as either metaphor or psychological projection. 'Conservatives', on the other hand, tended to downplay the material, interpreting the powers as fantastical monsters without making the necessary links to the powers of racism, militarism, nationalism or poverty.

How do we engage with our structures in a manner which is both material and spiritual? First, we must recognise our tendency to separate these two dimensions, and imagine they can be addressed separately. An example is when we analyse our decline in purely material terms, as being about the loss of numbers or finance, and fail to comprehend its spiritual dimensions. Often we compound this problem by attempting to fix an issue which is both material and spiritual in a singularly material way (through, for example, the reconfiguration of structures, or the closure of buildings). Not only does such an approach fail to address the whole of the problem, it also makes it worse.

This loss of the material–spiritual connection also occurs by more subtle means. Following an extensive survey of the literature of church renewal, from that produced in the 1970s to the present, pastors Andy Root and Blair Bertrand have observed that so far we have failed to find the method which will deliver lasting change. This may be because we have yet to locate the correct approach and must carry on searching, or it may be because every method suffers from the same fundamental flaw.

Many of these strategic methods (or 'methodologies' if we wish to sound more grand) actually took their initial vocabulary from the Church (vision and mission being the two most obvious examples) but returned that vocabulary back to the Church in a disenchanted form. Consequently, these approaches to church renewal subconsciously reinforce Secularism's core assumption: that there is no god or, if there is a god, then such a god is far off and only interested in the outcomes, but not the methods, of this kind of structural work (the god of civic society we met earlier). Yes, we may pray before we begin, and our strategies may even deploy Christian language, but fundamentally the tools of our structural work commonly reinforce the belief that 'this is down to us'. Therefore, Root and Bertrand conclude that 'instead of helping the Church', these approaches worsen our predicament 'by driving us deeper into the secular age we find ourselves in'.[7]

The temptation at this point is to ignore completely contemporary strategic thinking, but this in effect would be like ignoring the best ideas in medicine or the arts. And we would be attempting to address the sin of denying the spiritual by doing the opposite: denying the material. Instead, we need both, we need to re-enchant the world of strategy, and do what the book of Proverbs did; to hold the best strategic thinking of the age, and its own homegrown wisdom, within the paradigm of faith.[8] This can be done by reimagining those staples of the strategic world: vision, mission, timelines and values.

Our visions should be actual visions, and not three-line 'vision statements'. Biblical visions are often fantastical (Daniel and Revelation), troubling (Jeremiah), seemingly impossible (Isaiah) and lengthy (all of the above). They are like Martin Luther King's 'I have a dream' speech, which contained a searing critique of racist structures alongside its inspiring ideals. It is these kinds of prophetic visions which will genuinely inspire our strategic work.

Mission statements[9] will remain important in focusing our efforts. There are several scriptural examples of these (e.g. Luke 4:18–19; Matt. 28:19–20; John 20:21; Eph. 3:8–9) and, unlike visions, such Biblical mission statements are often concise. However, by themselves, these statements are insufficient, because they emphasise what we as humans are to do, and generally omit the action of God (an omission which, lest we forget, is a fundamental move of the secular age). Root and Bertrand helpfully suggest that mission statements should be paired with 'watchwords' – short phrases which draw attention to divine presence and action. They cite the example of Martin Luther King's experience during a particularly dark moment in the early days of the American civil rights movement when he heard God asking him to stand and to receive the word: 'When there is no way, I'll make a way.'[10] This watchword did much to sustain not only King, but also the wider movement. It is not hard to detect such watchwords in the New Testament; for example, 'It is through many persecutions that we must enter the kingdom of God' (Acts 14:22), 'My grace is sufficient for you, for power is made perfect in weakness' (2 Cor. 12:9) and 'Jesus is Lord' (Rom. 10:9). By combining mission statements with watchwords, we constantly remind ourselves that mission is a task which is both human and divine.

The timelines of contemporary project management are inherently focused on efficiency because 'time is money'; but God, it would appear, often prefers a different tempo. In the scriptures, God invents two forms of time: *chronos* (clock time) and *kairos* (appropriate time). Though *chronos* matters, the most significant moments in the Gospels often happen when Jesus moves to the rhythm of *kairos*, and usually to the considerable frustration of the disciples. In the work of the Church, we are not to ignore *chronos*, but we must also trust and wait for *kairos*. Sometimes this will mean moving quickly (as when the Israelites had to leave Egypt) but often this will entail considerable periods of waiting. Such waiting is not waste, for God works in the waiting, in a way which cannot happen when only *chronos* dictates our pace.

Like mission statements, value statements are not uncommon in the New Testament; Paul's fruits of the Spirit (love, joy, peace and patience, kindness, generosity, faithfulness, gentleness and self-control – Gal. 5:22) being a prime example. This list would not look out of place in any congregation's statements of values – or indeed in many secular organisations' statement of values.

But how many would be brave enough to consciously watch for Paul's corresponding 'works of the flesh' (even the 'milder' ones such as impurity, envy or carousing – Gal. 5:18–21)? To recognise these is to admit that there are instincts within us which are darker than the nobler values we are more ready to name. There is, though, something healthy in naming our 'shadow values': for (as any student of Jungian psychology knows) it is in our shadow that we often find the keys to our better selves. Without such honesty, we will be more tempted to hide, and when our darker behaviours emerge (as inevitably they will) we will be less able to confront them.

In this, we must say a special word about 'adaptive change' which frequently appears in more recent work on church transformation.[11] Based on the insights of leadership thinkers Ronald Heifetz and Marty Linsky, 'adaptive change' concerns the unknown – and often uncertain – processes of deep change which are required when we must adapt to a new environment. This approach has the potential to be of considerable importance in a Church which must learn to adapt to a secular age. Furthermore, many of its central movements concerning identity, trust, risk and values have always been integral to the life of faith. But there is one key warning, which is this: if any form of change, including 'adaptive change', is not grounded in divine and transformative encounter with the God who is God (as we have previously seen), then, whatever short-term successes may be achieved, we will also be drawn away from our true identity. Even the best approaches to strategic change must be grounded in God's presence and must consciously reject the disenchanted assumptions of the secular age.

Wrestling

In reminding ourselves that structures are material and spiritual, we will also have to recall that this will involve wrestling. In the mid-2000s, Tod Bolsinger had achieved something extremely rare: he had led organisational change within his congregation and his region of the PC(USA) and, given his track record, he was asked to lead a programme of national change. Over the next three years, Bolsinger and his team made all the right strategic moves and produced a set of proposals which, they hoped, might enable significant transformation. However, a few weeks before their report was due to be approved, Bolsinger began to notice a change in the wind. His calls were not being returned and he was being avoided at meetings. He soon deduced that, caught up within wider denominational forces, support for his team's report had begun to evaporate and it was indeed rejected on the floor of the PC(USA)'s General Assembly.

In despair, one young leader asked Bolsinger, 'What shall we do now?' Bolsinger replied, 'Go back home and build the best congregation you possibly can.' In other words, leave the national alone; the best we can do is concentrate on our local context.

Bolsinger's advice is not unattractive. Many church leaders, after years of frustration with regional and national structures, have reached the same conclusion. However, speaking to Tod Bolsinger now, he would modify the advice he gave back in 2012 and encourage 'potential change agents to spend *most* of their energy working to transform their own congregations; while still sharing what they are learning and maintaining relationships with those who are working in larger structures'.

I too still believe in working within all of our structures, despite all the inherent difficulties. Why? Partly because of the ability of such powers to deliver widespread and long-lasting change, but also because the New Testament calls us to wrestle with even the darkest powers, not to leave them alone.

Probably the most potent passage in this regard is Paul's teaching in Ephesians 6:10–20: declaring that we do not wrestle against flesh and blood (i.e. no scapegoating) but against darker powers (we should note that in the New Testament not all powers are dark, but those in Ephesians 6 most definitely are). Knowing this, we are called to be strong, to don the armour of God, to stand firm and to pray.

Where there are structures in our churches which continually break people, which continually bring out the worst of our behaviours, which leave behind them a trail of disillusionment and broken dreams, then these are precisely the places where we may be called to wrestle, fight and pray[12] and, having 'done all', to achieve little more perhaps than be left standing. With practical, functional eyes, we would say such endeavour was pointless, but faith and hope will open us up to a deeper purpose, for this struggle against the powers, it would appear, is closely linked to making known the mystery of the gospel (Eph. 3:9, 10; 6:19).

Questions

Much in this chapter avoids concrete 'recipes' (in fact, 'beware of concrete recipes' might be one of its principal cautions). Instead, it summons us to community discernment, to wait, to watch, to heed prophetic voices and to weigh their words (1 Cor. 14:29), to try, to fail, to keep waiting, to keep watching and to pray and to pray and to pray. Here are some questions which may enable such discernment:

1 What are our structures?
2 What are their material powers? (i.e. What can they visibly do?)
3 What is their spiritual power? (i.e. What is their invisible effect?)
4 How do we empower others?
5 Who else has power?
6 Who do we blame?
7 How do our structures embody community?
8 What is our vision (and, if we do not have one, then wait)?
9 What is our mission?
10 What are our watchwords?
11 Where do we work to clock time?
12 Where do we wait for appropriate time?
13 What are our values?
14 What are our shadow values?
15 Where do we wrestle?
16 In all of this, how shall we pray?

When Structures Work

I want to end this chapter by relating one of my favourite stories about structure and renewal, a story I frequently return to when the work of structure becomes dispiriting, and abandonment seems tempting. About fifteen years ago, I was involved in a meeting to explore our denomination's support for a fledgling youth organisation, one with a vision to work with young people from some of Scotland's poorest communities in their local contexts and in the outdoors. At first, I was unconvinced: Scotland already had numerous Christian outdoor organisations, why did we need another?

However, the vision and wisdom of two individuals, Alex and Neil, and the prophetic insight of a minister called Irene Bristow, undermined my doubts. Irene, a veteran of ministry in Scotland's poorest communities, declared this to be a *kairos* moment, a unique opportunity for the Church to engage with the disabling powers of economic deprivation, and the marginalisation of young people. I was sceptical as to Irene's uninhibited rhetoric, but this was an area where our Church was failing and, in offering limited support for a pilot, what did we have to lose?

With a small amount of initial funding, and the provision of office space and governance support, 'The GKExperience' (or, more simply, 'GK')[13] was born. In these early days it could not have functioned without the Church's support, and through a huge amount of work from Alex and her team the project began to flourish. But there were also many desperate moments and not a few desperate prayers.

In the years since, community building has remained at the heart of GK's work, as has an attention to structures, often with a degree of imagination and invention. The 'Green hoodies' (named after the item of clothing they each wear) are young leaders who have grown through the work and now help to deliver the programmes, while continuing to receive regular support. They bring a real-life perspective on the challenges which GK's young people face. Eventually, the Green hoodies may become 'Blue hoodies', the project's senior leaders.

In order that our denominational support departments could see, for themselves, the value of what they enabled, a group of young people from GK were asked to run a team-building day for some of our church offices' management team. At that event, senior executives were given assessments of their leadership skills by entirely unfazed teenagers and also, after a grandparent picked up his phone and heard some terrible news, those same executives became the group of listeners that he, in that moment, desperately needed.

Fifteen years after that initial feasibility meeting, I attended Alex's wedding: it was full of young people and their families, many of whose lives had been changed by GK. In a marquee, pitched on the side of a hill on the island of Skye, wedding dresses were surrounded by a joyous affirming community. Irene Bristow had been right: the discussions in 2010 had indeed been a *kairos* moment. Not long after that meeting, Irene died of cancer, but at Alex's wedding I could only give thanks at being allowed to witness her words come true.

GK is an endeavour which has been both spiritual and material, and could not have existed without its own structures, or our Church's wider structures. For good powerful structures are what our boldest visions always require. That is why, as the New Testament testifies (Col. 1:15–23), Christ not only created the powers, but also reconciled them through the cross. I believe that on an exuberant dance floor on the island of Skye, I was once given a glimpse of that redemption.

PART 2

The Gifts

9

Charisms

Adaptive Change

A monkey cannot become a caterpillar, a fir tree cannot become a rose bush, and even the largest of mushrooms cannot hope to become a whale. Just as in the adaption of species, so will an adapting church retain much of its original character. In the changes ahead, a mainline church will become a new form of mainline church; it will not become a conservative, Catholic or Orthodox congregation. It must become new, and it must remain authentically itself. For all of its radical nature, the change we need is not a complete revision, but rather a profound adaption of what we currently are, an adaption which enables us to live within a new world. In the vocabulary of evolution, we will retain much (but not all) of our existing DNA. Or, to use language from the scriptures and the early life of the Church, we will retain many of our *charisms*: our unique gifts which form the shape of who we are.[1]

Trusting Our Gifts

The importance of appreciating and developing our own gifts emerges in the story of one of the most remembered (and revered) moments in the history of the twentieth-century Scottish Church, the Tell Scotland evangelistic movement. In the early 1950s, many Scottish church leaders had begun to notice a change in the cultural wind: the Church did not seem to matter to the Scottish people as it once had. Coming together across denominational divides, a broad group of Scottish churches launched Tell Scotland, a campaign to share the Christian gospel with everyone in Scotland.

Initially this movement aimed to develop teams of local evangelists who would share the gospel in their own communities, building on an approach that had been successfully pioneered – in his previous parish – by Tom Allan, the Field Director of Tell Scotland. However, in early 1954, six months after the campaign's official launch, Allan was becoming increasingly concerned that local churches were not yet ready for the task, and so he persuaded the movement's steering committee to invite the then upcoming American evangelist Billy Graham to lead a crusade in Scotland – the 'All Scotland Crusade'. This decision was not without controversy, with protests that Billy Graham's style did not align with Scottish culture. Some people argued that Graham paid insufficient attention to social justice,[2] and that Tell Scotland's initial emphasis on local evangelism needed to be given more of a chance. A number of key leaders left the movement because of the decision to invite Billy Graham and the movement's broad theological unity would be lost for ever.

Despite these misgivings, the All Scotland Crusade of 1955 was initially viewed as a euphoric success and is still remembered by many who were there as one of the most important moments in their own journey of faith. Following the Crusade, there was also a surge in church attendance; however, over the following months, many new converts drifted away; 'there was nothing which gripped them', said one of Tell Scotland's follow-up reports. With great disappointment, the movement's leaders soon concluded that the Crusade had failed to meet its principal aim: of transforming the Scottish Church. Religious trends returned to their previous patterns and the steep numerical decline of the Scottish Church (in particular, of the mainline Church) would soon become very apparent.[3]

What subsequent analysis has shown, however, is that, despite Tom Allan's concerns, Tell Scotland's initial locally based approach to mission had actually been working. In 1954 – that is, after the launch of the Tell Scotland movement but prior to the All Scotland Crusade – the number of new members in Scottish churches did see a remarkable rise. Locally based mission, for all its challenges and lack of apparent success, was actually working. However, after the movement shifted its focus to arena-based evangelism (no matter how temporary it intended this shift to be), the emphasis on local evangelism was never recaptured. The noted evangelist of the day, D. P. Thomson, reflecting on the effectiveness of Tell Scotland, later wrote that the 'parish and regional work of evangelism in which the local forces were being both trained and used at every stage would have proved far more effective and fruitful in the long run'.[4]

The story of the Tell Scotland crusade, back in the early days of Secularisation, provides some fruitful lessons: the importance of retaining Christian unity; the essential breadth to mission – of both personal salvation and social justice; and the effectiveness of locally based approaches to mission and evangelism. There is always great value in learning from approaches being adopted in other contexts, but we must not be seduced by them, and we must always cherish and develop the gifts we have already been given, even if their value takes some time to become apparent.

In focusing on our gifts, we will move from what Old Testament theologian Walter Brueggemann calls an 'economy of scarcity' to an 'economy of abundance'. Reflecting on the story of Exodus, Brueggemann notes that the myth of scarcity abounded in Egypt: it was scarcity which got frightened (even when it had enough); this mindset hoarded but did not share, bred anxiety, and turned the people into overworked slaves. Abundance, on the other hand, is the economy which celebrates manna in the desert, the gift whose name literally means 'what is it?' and whose mysteries we are invited to explore. Abundance confidently gathers, knows it has enough, and knows when to rest. Scarcity fixates on our deficits; abundance knows that we have everything we need. Scarcity breeds fear, abundance assures us of a future. Scarcity fears abandonment, abundance knows that God is near.[5]

In the letters of the New Testament, its churches are frequently reminded of the variety and abundance of the gifts they have received (e.g. Rom. 12:6; 1 Cor 1:7; 3:21; Eph. 4:7–8;

James 1:17). In the subversive economy of abundance, even the poorest of churches can delight in their gifts and live with risky generosity (2 Cor. 8:2, 15). Indeed, our current season of loss may well be the very thing which enables us to flourish in the abundance of God.

Our gifts also profoundly shape us. They hold us true to our identity, while also leading us into radical change. Each of our gifts must be noticed, appreciated and received; they must also be pursued. And though these are given for the building up of the Church, they are also given for the whole of the world. Gifts also have a sacramental quality; they lead us into divine encounter which, as we have already seen, is the most important movement in the renewal of the mainline Church. Here, then, in the remainder of this book, is a portrait of seven defining mainline gifts: what they look like, how they have shaped our story, and how they might be pursued in the current age:

1 Connection
2 Community
3 Scripture
4 Justice
5 Land
6 Song
7 Stillness

10

Connection

'We are "all over" number three,' said one of the most esteemed leaders in our denomination. He was referring to the 'Five Marks of Mission', those five signatures which concisely express the breadth of mission, and which have become prevalent in many parts of the Church since they were first developed in the Church of England in the 1980s.

Mark number three is 'To respond to human need with loving service'. We in the mainline are very good at this: we run and host foodbanks, community cafés, community gardens, dementia support groups, parent and toddler groups, men's 'sheds', and women's groups. This need is not confined to our own local communities; we are strong supporters of many charities, including a number which are not specifically faith based. Amnesty International, the Campaign for Nuclear Disarmament and Extinction Rebellion would be considerably impoverished without the many Christians who support their work.

Mainliners are particularly good at reaching across the boundaries of the Church and connecting with those in our local communities, regardless of faith background. This ability to connect with non-members is sometimes referred to as 'bridging social capital'. A 2004 study of North American churches confirmed that bridging social capital was indeed more abundant in mainline churches than in conservative ones[1] (the conservative churches tended to possess stronger internal bonds, a phenomenon which we will explore in the next chapter).

Mainliners exercise their bridging social capital both as part of official Church organisations, and as individuals. A recent survey of my own regional council, for example, found that in comparison to the general population, elected councillors were more likely to belong to mainline churches than most other Christian denominations (the exception was the Roman Catholic Church), and that Christians as a whole were far more likely to become councillors than those who described their religious affiliation as 'none'. Mainliners are good at bridging with their communities (and, before we congratulate ourselves too much, Roman Catholics, at least according to this particular survey, are even better).

The Gospel for All

Why do mainliners have this deep desire to connect with those outside their congregation, to be a society which, in Archbishop William Temple's famous words, 'exists for the benefit of those who are not its members'? At heart is our belief that in Jesus Christ, God is doing something radically new, not only in the Church, but in the world; that the resurrection of Jesus inaugurates not just a new church, but a new creation and that, through him, the embrace of God is made available to all. As Jesus says in John 12:32, 'And I, when I am lifted up from the earth, will draw all people to myself.'

Very early in the history of the Protestant Reformation, the movement divided into two: the Magisterial Reformation which sat close to, or even within, the apparatus of the state, and the Radical Reformation which rejected all secular authority. It was the Radical Reformation which tended to identify with the scriptural notion of the divine remnant: the notion that the gospel would only ever be believed by a relatively small number. The churches of the Magisterial Reformation, however, identified with the instinct that the Good News of Jesus was for every person and every part of society. Even John Calvin, whose later followers were parodied as praying that 'God sent one to heaven and ten to hell, all for thy glory',[2] believed that the grace of Christ 'belongs to a greater number than the condemnation contracted by the first man'.[3]

Believing that the gospel was for all, the churches of the Magisterial Reformation worked closely with the state (very

often too closely) and sought to reform, and therefore connect with, the whole of society. As the Magisterial churches
morphed into the churches of the mainline, this *charism* for
connection was retained.

In believing that the kingdom is bigger than the Church and
that the mission of God leaps over the boundaries marked by
narrow religion, mainliners are often passionate about relating
to those outside their number. There is, though, one important
caveat to this mainline love of bridge-building. We can make
bridges when the currency is social justice, or personal well-
being, or the provision of shared community resources. However,
we find these connections considerably more difficult in the
arena of overt faith.

When it comes to the Five Marks of Mission, 'we are all over
number three', and we do not do too badly with four and five
(justice and the environment), but with numbers one and two
('proclaiming the Good News' and 'baptising and nurturing
new believers') we struggle. This is true in traditional mainline
churches and also in the new worshipping communities they
have planted. Recently, I heard a national coordinator for such
communities observe that 'we are good at walking around a
forest and sensing our spirituality, but how do we move from
this to discipleship in the Christian faith?'

This disconnect is mirrored in our surrounding communities.
People may drink coffee in our cafes, attend choir practice in
our halls, and support our campaigns to alleviate poverty. But
when it comes to our faith, our beliefs and our spirituality, we
are judged to be either irrelevant or, to be totally frank, boring.
To understand this difficulty, we need to explore a little further
the phenomenon of religious boredom.

The Height of Scottish Church Boredom

For millions of Scots, Presbyterian boredom and disconnection
are personified in one man: the Revd I. M. Jolly. Played by
legendary comic Rikki Fulton, the Revd Jolly was based on too
many Church of Scotland ministers, whose sincere but dour

platitudes had been boring the Scottish population for decades. Appearing on the Hogmanay[4] sketch show *Scotch and Wry* from the late 1970s to the early 1990s, the humour of Jolly's monologues lay in their disconnection, a disconnection from which Jolly himself seemed utterly oblivious. His name said Jolly, but he was miserable; when attempting comedy, he was humourless; when attempting seriousness, he was hilarious. His parishioners didn't understand him and his wife seemed to avoid him. Only when the religious façade slipped, when Jolly began to swear at having endured a terrible week, or emerged in delight after a visit to a Museum of Horrors, did we sense the real human being underneath, however dark and shadowy that individual might be.

The reason that *Scotch and Wry*'s huge audience laughed at Jolly, and why he became the show's most memorable character, was because his spirit was so pervasive in the life of Scottish culture. Scots immediately recognised him from their school assemblies, their funerals and weddings, and their occasional attendance at Sunday morning worship. However, the disconnection epitomised by Jolly would exact a heavy cost. *Scotch and Wry* featured no fewer than seven Jolly-esque religious characters. Just over a decade after its heyday, the coveted Hogmanay comedy slot was occupied by another much-loved sketch show: *Chewin' the Fat*; among its cast of memorable characters, the number who were religious was precisely zero.

The Revd I. M. Jolly stands testament to the cost of all-encompassing disconnectedness; of a man who was disconnected from his people, but also, it appeared, from himself and from God. Within the faith, there seemed no scope for Jolly to become himself; he only became authentic when leaving the world of faith behind. This begs the question, is this always inevitable? Can we stay true to ourselves, and to our faith? Can we remain connected to ourselves, our neighbours and to God within the community of belief? The answer to this question involves the daring risk of faithful authenticity; and to learn more of this we must move from the fictional Revd I. M. Jolly to the Old Testament book of Job.

Job

Some of the most boring chapters in the Bible are probably in Job. Before being accused of heresy, I should add that I believe them to be deliberately so. The story is that Job, an individual of unimpeachable virtue, has had his livestock, his assets and his family destroyed in a series of disasters, before he himself is struck by an agonising skin disease. In the following days, he is joined by three friends who, after seeing the immensity of his suffering, weep and wail, tear their clothes, and sit in silence for a week.

Then Job, in increasingly extreme and uncensored language, complains to God at the severity and injustice of his plight. His friends, now horrified at Job's intemperate vitriol, take it upon themselves to defend God, and to castigate their friend in a series of highly wearying speeches – speeches which I tentatively suggest are deliberately boring. When a fourth companion, the precocious Elihu, launches into a six-chapter monologue towards the end of the book, the reader's patience is severely tried.

However, despite their relentless and unsympathetic verbiage, none of these speeches are, it first seems, scripturally incorrect. Their language could have come from the psalms, and they could claim at least some Biblical justification from the book of Deuteronomy. This is of no consolation to the enraged Job who describes his friends as 'miserable comforters' (Job 16:2).

At the end of the story, though, we discover that not only have these speeches earned the ire of Job and engendered the weariness of the reader; God too has been unimpressed, twice declaring that these friends had 'not spoken of me what is right, as my servant Job has' (Job 42:7). This, for me, is one of the most surprising and revelatory statements in the whole of the Bible: the apparent orthodoxy of Job's friends is condemned, while the intemperate accusations of Job receive divine affirmation. We can only conclude that it was not the doctrinal content of the friends' speeches which were so problematic, but rather their disconnectedness: from their friend, from God (twice God emphasises that they have not spoken rightly of 'me') and, because they were playing a religious part, from themselves. It was through this triple disconnection, from others, from God, and from themselves, that the friends' speeches were rendered utterly, utterly, utterly boring.

If we take our diagnosis from the book of Job, the root cause of years of Scottish boredom in Presbyterian pews was not the result of inadequate cushioning, antiquated music, nor even sermonic word count (however unhelpful these may have been); the root cause was disconnection: from others, from ourselves, and from God.

However, the book of Job gives us some hope. For it seems to teach that when we courageously express ourselves, when we authentically voice our own experience and tell God what we genuinely believe (however unpalatable that may be to conventional religious sensibilities), then our speech becomes utterly compelling. And though God may argue back (Job 38:2) with poetry of God's own, there is something profoundly truthful about the whole exchange. From all this daring authenticity and deep connection, something new emerges, a new form of faithful speech or, in the language of the psalmist, 'a new song' (Ps. 33:3; 40:3; 96:1; 98:1; 144:9; 149:1).

Crafting and giving voice to this faithful, daring and poetic language is our great missional calling. We cannot fall back on the platitudes of the past (no matter how scripturally justified they may be), we have to reach for something truthful and new. This is our work, to compose and sing a new song which is truthful to our communities, to ourselves and to the faith within us.

A New Connection

This 'new song' is witnessed in the evangelism of the apostle Paul. For Paul, the gospel had revealed a new understanding of humanity, the world, and God. It was expressing the fact that, in Christ, Israel's God had entered the world and in his life, crucifixion and resurrection, had inaugurated a new creation. This is a creation in which sins are forgiven, the darkest powers defeated; the desires of sinful human nature are put to death; and through the Holy Spirit we as individuals and communities are made new in love and called to hope.

From this new-found sense of connection to others, God and self, Paul speaks and writes with a whole new language, honing metaphors which were drawn from the life of the home, the slave market and the law courts. With new interpretations of the Old Testament and analogies to parenthood and human love, he took a gospel which had first been proclaimed among the peasants of Galilee and refashioned its message for the urban communities of Asia Minor, Greece and Rome. We should not underestimate the imagination and depth of what he achieved: within the space of twenty years, Paul had forged a new vocabulary for salvation which would shape the Church's life for the following two millennia. Avoiding platitude or cliché, but not exuberance, hyperbole or poetry, he crafted a message which proved utterly compelling to those who were ready to hear. Like the psalmist, he had learned to sing a new song.[5]

Singing a New Song

Learning to sing a new song is a demanding calling. In 2008, Ricky Ross, singer and songwriter with the iconic Scottish band Deacon Blue, had a revelation. Life in that year already had much happening; it was what Irene Bristow, cited in the previous chapter, might have called a *kairos* moment. Deacon Blue had a superb back catalogue including music which helped form the backdrop to my own teenage years: not least Lorraine McIntosh's 'whooo-oooo-ooooo-ooooo' in 'Real Gone Kid' and that iconic anthem to universal human worth, 'Dignity'. But at this point the band's newer material was, in Ross's own words 'half-hearted at best'.[6] Without the energy that comes from fresh creativity, touring was proving to be a less than happy experience.

While supporting and watching another legendary Scottish band, Simple Minds, Ross had an epiphany: here was a band who remained connected to their audience while 'constantly updating themselves' and 'holding to the essence of what they'd always been'. This, Ross realised, was something he wanted again for Deacon Blue.

The band had to learn to sing a new song. How did this happen? They held to the calling of that initial *kairos* moment, they took risks, employed their long-honed artistry, and were patient. They went deep into who they were, told stories which inspired them, and worked on music which they loved. This was not a set process, but obedience to a sometimes-exhausting calling: the sense that if you don't do this, then part of you withers and dies, but if you do it, if you keep faith and have courage, then there is no joy like it.

It's the same for the Church, we are going to have to work at this, to go deep, to trust in our gifts, to keep trying, to be patient. If we avoid this, we'll wither, but if we somehow trust that God might be in this, that we might be called to this, then we will get there. We will find the new song; we will find our voice.

My first awareness of Deacon Blue's renaissance came many years later, in mid-2020 when, not long after the first Covid lockdown was imposed, my friend Tim phoned and asked, 'Neil, have you listened to Deacon Blue's new album? It's incredible.' That album, *City of Love*, with its celebration of human connection, released just before a lockdown in which we missed that connection and yearned for it like never before, became an essential part of my soundtrack to 2020, just as the band's earlier songs had been to my teenage years.

This combination of work, gift and calling is also the testimony of my friend Foy. In his early twenties, encouraged by his dad and with the knowledge that he had an incredible voice, he performed all over Northern Ireland and further afield, singing other people's songs. But one night, while performing in the Canary Islands, he kept hearing a new song, 'Crying In The Night'. The song wouldn't go away and so, for the first time, Foy sang his own song and sensed a new connection with his audience.

Tragically, the next morning, Foy got a call with terrible news: his dad had died the night before. For Foy, the night he was given his gift is now indelibly linked with the moment of his biggest loss. Over the years, Foy has written hundreds of songs. He is remarkably gifted at crafting words and sound. He can also work hard. During days in the studio, he will work and work and work. Through frustration and tiredness, he will continue to work until the song emerges. Sometimes he works alone, but very often with others, and he has a tremendous gift for encouraging the talents of fellow songwriters (including some who have had stellar careers). Many people have covered his songs but the greatest nights are when he sings them himself, with wholehearted and full-throated conviction, and the song lives and those who hear are taken to another place.

In the secular age we are called, as a church, to sing a new gospel song in what Walter Brueggemann calls a 'prose-flattened world'[7]: to bear witness to the God who comes close; who weaves a story; who embraces our whole and hurting selves; who rescues from death; who promises hope; who prepares a way; who shapes our being; who calls us to love of enemy and neighbour; who contends for justice; who moves with artistry, kindness and grace; who embraces us without limit or condition. To find expression for this gospel, to find our voice, is demanding work – we do not know what will emerge and it will take much time. So we must not be distracted or delay, now is the moment to begin.

Re-bridging

The Revd Adam Smallbone, titular character of the 2010s sitcom *Rev*,[8] is, on the surface at least, very different from the Revd I. M. Jolly: one is a young Anglican priest on an inner-city estate, the other is a middle-aged Presbyterian in an affluent suburb. Yet they both share the same disappointment: that the life of a clergyman has not been all they had hoped it would be; and both of them experience a loneliness which is exacerbated by the distance between their public role and their inner selves. Where they most differ is in their willingness to voice such disappointment: Jolly, with his cheerless platitudes, sounds like one of Job's friends; Smallbone, with his embittered questions and furious complaints, sounds more like Job himself.

At the end of *Rev*'s first season, Smallbone has spiralled into a depression which, to his wife, looks worryingly deeper than the usual bi-annual crises in which 'he believes in God, he's just not sure if God believes in him'. Having got drunk and made a fool of himself at a party, Smallbone gets into an altercation with some local youths, and is picked up by the police.

Thinking he is being driven to the cells, Smallbone is surprised instead to be led into a block of high-rise flats, with the policeman asking him to perform the last rites for a woman who is about to die. Smallbone refuses to go in. 'I don't think you've got the right man,' he protests, 'I'm not sure I'm strong and able.' Refusing to take 'no' for an answer, the policeman persists: 'this woman is in great pain, she's been hanging on, she wants release … now are you her vicar or not?'

Leaning against a bare concrete pillar, unshaven and disconsolate, Smallbone goes deep into himself and remembers the verse from his ordination service: 'I heard the voice of the Lord say, "Whom shall I send and who will go for us?", and I said, "Here I am, send me."' At this, Smallbone finds just enough faith to enter the flat and to celebrate the Eucharist with a dying woman and her husband.

It's a scene which nearly always brings me to tears. I remember the first time I watched it during a crisis in my own faith, and how, days later, I too prayed with barely sufficient faith at the bedside of a dying man. It is a scene which depicts in comic extremes the doubt we all carry, that we can never be evangelists of the gospel: 'we believe in God, we're just not sure if God believes in us'. And yet, for all his frailty and self-doubt, in that moment at a dying woman's bedside, Adam Smallbone was given just enough to live up to his ordination promise, to connect with himself, with two strangers and with God. This was not an easy gift, but it also brought him back to life.

May we in the mainline also rediscover our essential connections, share bread with a world still hungry for the taste of God, and in this demanding vocation also find ourselves.

11

Community

Lydia Sohn, Lynsey Brennan and Lynn McChlery are each mainline ministers in growing congregations: Lydia in California; Lynsey and Lynn in Scotland. All three are gifted leaders of worship. They share a passion for community: communities which contain young and old; long-established stalwarts and inquisitive newcomers; Sunday morning worshippers, parish allies and those in the blurry in-between.

In her early thirties, Lydia Sohn, a Korean American, was posted to a United Methodist congregation whose members were ethnically and culturally very different from her. Her biggest concern was the difference in age: most of her new congregants were many decades older than she was. To Lydia, at that point, older people had interests, passions and concerns which were disconcertingly different from her own. However, this image was shattered on the day that a woman in her eighties tearfully shared that she had fallen in love with another man, a man who would never be able to return her affections because he himself was married. To Lydia, this felt like the kind of conversation she might have expected to have with a woman in her teenage years, not one in her eighties. Determined to discover more, Lydia embarked on a research project among the eldest people in her congregations, those in their nineties. She asked them the biggest questions about their lives: did they still crave sex, did they still harbour dreams, when had been their best moments?

Looking back now, Lydia recognises that she had two large preconceptions about older people: that they were either sage and detached, or jaded and disillusioned. Neither of these turned out to be true. Those 90-year-old parishioners had the exact same dreams, regrets and desires (including for sex) as those in every other adult age group. Lydia also realised that her anxieties about connecting with those significantly older than her were rooted in her own fear of ageing, but as she conducted her research this fear dissipated. In discovering that our passions do not diminish with age, the thought of growing old became considerably less fearful.

Lydia was also bowled over by how grateful the participants were to take part in the research; so rarely were they given the opportunity for this kind of exchange. As one participant said to her, 'I wish that my granddaughter could hear me having this conversation with you now.'

Almost ten years later, Lydia retains the same curiosity and interest in people of all ages which emerged when she had conducted that survey. This infectious attention to each individual has spread throughout her current congregation and its intergenerational nature has become one of its defining characteristics. Regardless of age, ethnicity or background, every single member of her congregation is someone who is seen.

For six months, in the Glasgow suburb of Eaglesham, Lynn McChlery laboured with her elders and members to uncover a vision for the future. After lengthy research exercises, extensive reading, continuous prayer and countless conversations, what emerged was remarkably simple: DNA groups – with DNA standing for Discipleship, Nurture and Action. Each group contained three people who, preferably, had not previously known one another particularly well. 'Stretch out your two hands,' she told her congregation. 'Grab who you can, and the three of you will be a DNA group.' The format of these sessions would be simple: fifteen minutes of conversation (Nurture), fifteen minutes of prayer and Bible engagement (Discipleship), and fifteen minutes identifying a specific Action (this can be anything – from investigating a social issue to tidying a neighbour's garden). The groups would meet exactly once a week (regardless of time or place, they would meet with all three members present) and disband after six weeks. Later, new groups would be formed, with different configurations of members.

To Lynn's great delight, in Eaglesham and now in her current congregation in Auchterarder, these groups have flourished. Initially people were anxious, but soon discovered new connections between faith, life and one another. Such is the congregation's enthusiasm that often they now invite non-churchgoers to become members.

For Lynsey Brennan, relationships in Dundonald are developed through weekly worship, her church's community-engagement project ('Floyds' – named after her cat); and one-to-one 'faith walks' around a local reservoir with its stunning views. Lynsey is open about the struggles she has faced, and continues to face, in her own life; this enables different people to connect with and relate to her. Having done much of her own research into the nature of Secularism, she firmly maintains that people today are 'craving a sense of belonging to something bigger than themselves and are attracted to church communities based on "agape" love'. Her main goal is 'not to grow the church but to remember the first mission of God, which is to be fully human with each other, showing kindness, care and respect to all'. This, she maintains, cannot be emulated other than by the 'Spirit of the living Triune God'. Lynsey has witnessed huge congregational growth, with many members of the addiction-support community and single-parent families becoming members; essential to this has been the welcome offered by the existing congregation.

Programmes are important but, for Lynn, Lydia and Lynsey, far more important are the habitual practices of hospitality, conversation and connection. Numerical growth happens to be taking place in this current season, but as Lynn remarks: 'Never before in my ministry have I experienced growth like this, and I don't expect to again.' Numerical growth is not what defines the health of their communities; what counts is depth of relationship, with (and these three connections keep reappearing) ourselves, others and God. Their stories illustrate several other key principles which are essential in fostering the health of our congregational communities.

Community is a Demanding Task

Fostering community is demanding, intensive and, sometimes, seemingly mundane work. When I ask Lydia how she builds community, I am surprised that her first answer is 'have a really good weekly newsletter'. But then I remember that Paul's early communities were also sustained by community letters so inspirational that they would later form half the books in the New Testament. I think too of the Aberdeen minister and leader of the evangelical Crieff Fellowship, William Still, who, in a ministry of over fifty years, sustained and inspired countless ministers and church members across Scotland and beyond with his regular correspondence. A former supervisor of mine, to whom 'Mr Still' had been *in loco parentis* while his parents had been overseas missionaries, tells of the piles of letters in the manse study most evenings, ready to be sent to correspondents around the world. This is the routine and diligent work of connection, involving texts, letters, calls and visits, which is essential to the growth of community.

Too often, though, the work of community is of an even more demanding nature. No community can avoid it: the negotiation of tension and conflict. In one of his most poignant passages (2 Cor. 11:23–30), the apostle Paul lists his privations: whipped, beaten and stoned; three times shipwrecked; frequently hungry, thirsty, cold and naked. And he adds, 'Besides other things, I am under daily pressure because of my anxiety for all the churches.' Remarkably for Paul, anxiety for his churches, whether these were under persecution or riven by internal conflict, was so painful that it bore comparison with being flogged or being shipwrecked. Even Paul, one of the most gifted community builders in Christian history, knew the pain and work of holding a community together.

Almost as dramatically, George MacLeod, renowned leader of the Iona Community, would speak of journeying back to Iona after trips away. Reaching the small village of Fionnphort on the island of Mull, he would look across the narrow sound to Iona and the famous Abbey – to me, one of the most beautiful views in all the world. But in that moment, however,

MacLeod's stomach would start to churn as he remembered all the tensions, challenges and disputes which awaited him. MacLeod, a decorated veteran of the First World War, would recall that this moment felt even worse than returning to the trenches. Even for the most celebrated of community builders, there are no short-cuts; the work of community is demanding.

Community Needs a Demanding Task

Also, said George MacLeod, 'Every community needs a demanding common task.' For his community, this had been the challenge of rebuilding a thirteenth-century Benedictine Abbey on one of Scotland's more remote islands, during an economic depression and a global war. As the work approached its seemingly miraculous completion, the Iona Community got ready to celebrate, but also became concerned. What would they do now? The task had needed them, but they had also needed the task. Going ahead, they would need to find a purpose which made similarly exacting demands.

This essential relationship between community and task was a continued feature of Israel's exodus from Egypt. At first, the task was obvious – to get out – but it became harder to discern in the wilderness. However, as often happens in the desert, God provided. Here, as an example, is an excerpt from Exodus 36:

> ... make the tabernacle with ten curtains of fine twisted linen, and blue, purple, and crimson yarns; you shall make them with cherubim skilfully worked into them. The length of each curtain shall be twenty-eight cubits, and the width of each curtain four cubits; all the curtains shall be of the same size. Five curtains shall be joined to one another; and the other five curtains shall be joined to one another. You shall make loops of blue on the edge of the outermost curtain in the first set; and likewise you shall make loops on the edge of the outermost curtain in the second set. You shall make fifty loops on the one curtain ... You shall make fifty clasps of gold, and

join the curtains to one another with the clasps, so that the tabernacle may be one whole. (Exod. 26:1–6)

Not only do these extremely specific, and slightly exhausting, instructions continue for six chapters, but they are repeated – almost word-for-word – in the final part of the book. For the writer of Exodus, this was not 'mere tabernacle construction'; it receives the same degree of attention as the book's earlier accounts of plagues and fiery mountains. Why all this sewing, clasping, joining, carrying and making? And why was it deemed essential that such minutiae be recorded? It seems that the task, in all its detail, was remarkably important. To reach the promised land, it was vital that the community escape the chariots of Pharaoh and also vital that it twisted linen and sewed together curtains.

Ancient commentators often wrote that the tabernacle was a symbol of the whole universe. This applied both to its final form, and also to the work of creation. The construction of the tabernacle echoed the Genesis creation in the presence of the Spirit (Gen. 1:2 and Exod. 31:1–11 – especially striking since the Spirit is rarely explicitly mentioned in the Old Testament); the rhythm of 'Word' leading to 'Action'; and the completing act of Sabbath (Gen. 2:1–3 and Exod. 31:12–17). Both creations were also brought about by a community. In Genesis, creation is one of those rare Biblical instances when we are given insight into the community within God: 'Let us make humankind in our image,' says God to God's self in Genesis 1:26. In the desert, the whole community contributed materials, and all who were skilful contributed their labour (Exod. 35:10). In Genesis and Exodus, God and the Israelites are both depicted as communities who engage in a demanding common task.

Conversely, any attempt to reduce the demand of the common task is disastrous. When Aaron instantly produces a counterfeit god (Exod. 32:4), in a manner quite different from the prolonged and communal work of tabernacle construction, the community forgets its core identity and breaks down into false worship and senseless revelry. Rupturing relationship with their liberator God, thousands die, and huge restorative work is required to bring about some form of repair. Beware of the moments, this episode seems to teach, when we are tempted to cut short or individualise the demanding task to which our community is called.

Healthy Communities Bridge and Bond

In our last chapter, we encountered research which suggested that mainline churches tended to possess significant bridging social capital – the ability to forge links with those outside their own membership. The same research also discovered that conservative congregations tended to accumulate greater amounts of 'bonding social capital', the formation of strong relationships within their community.[1] However, true Christian community is never a choice between internal 'bonding' and external 'bridging'; healthy communities do both.

In order to better understand this double capacity, we require an insight which was so critical to the teaching of the German pastor Dietrich Bonhoeffer. In the 1930s, Bonhoeffer had formed two communities of theology students in which he repeatedly stressed that members of his communities were not to relate to one another through the 'human' bonds of mutual respect but through their common relationship with Christ. 'Our community with one another consists solely in what Christ has done to both of us,' he wrote.[2] When a community is bonded in Christ, its internal bonds are remarkably strong; but so too is its ability to bridge, because both sets of relationships no longer depend on conformity to some hidden code of merit, shared background or common social rank. Relationships are based solely on Christ, the one who unites across all human distinctions. Thus, true Christian community both bridges and bonds.

The bonds which Bonhoeffer helped forge in his communities proved to be remarkably resilient, not least through the unthinkable pressures of war. However, these strong internal bonds did not detract from, but rather enhanced, the relationships which Bonhoeffer and his students made with outsiders.

For Bonhoeffer himself, this was never more apparent than when he was imprisoned for the last two years of his life. Frequently, other prisoners spoke of his cheer, and asked to speak and pray with him.

In the last days of Bonhoeffer's life, crammed into the back of a clapped-out prison van and transported for hundreds of miles across Germany, he remained, in the words of one of the van's other occupants, 'very happy' and did a huge amount to keep some of his fellow prisoners from depression and anxiety. During this ordeal, Bonhoeffer spent hours sharing his faith and learning Russian from an atheist by the name of Wasily Kokorin. Upon reaching an abandoned schoolhouse, the other prisoners pressed Bonhoeffer to hold a service, but he resisted out of respect for Kokorin's atheism; only after Kokorin insisted that the service went ahead did Bonhoeffer conduct a deeply moving act of worship which, according to another prisoner, 'touched the hearts of us all'.

No sooner, though, had Bonhoeffer uttered his final prayer when two plain-clothed and sinister-looking individuals came into the room and said, 'Prisoner Bonhoeffer ... get ready to come with us!' After saying farewell to his fellow prisoners, Bonhoeffer departed with the words 'This is the end. For me the beginning of life.'[3]

Dietrich Bonhoeffer demonstrated that relationships which are rooted in Christ will also make profound connections with those outside the community of faith. It is less apparent, at least on first inspection, how this principle was manifest in the first Christian communities. We have already seen how Paul forged diverse communities with strong internal bonds, a subject on which he frequently wrote, urging his people to the heights of love (e.g. 1 Cor. 13) and describing them as the very body of Christ (e.g. 1 Cor. 12). However, he rarely explicitly urged his congregations to make connections with outsiders and his letters contain no instructions to conduct open-air rallies or engage in friendship evangelism. Why was this? It seems that for Paul there was no need to generate additional opportunity for outside contact; his assumption seems to have been that members of his churches were already in frequent contact with outsiders (Phil. 1:14, Col. 1:5–6), including during their acts of worship (1 Cor. 14:23). It doesn't seem to have occurred to him that his community would have become a disconnected sect.

Rather, Paul's primary concern seems to have been that, should an outsider wish to become a part of the Church, none of the criteria for belonging which were frequently adopted by the households, voluntary associations, and even the synagogues of his day would be applied in his Christian communities. So it was that bonds of social rank, mutual affinity, common identity (marked by outward signs such as circumcision and diet) and gender were to be of absolutely no consideration in his churches (Gal. 3:28; Col. 3:11). He ferociously opposed any attempt to use such criteria as a basis for membership or the establishment of an internal hierarchy (Gal. 2:14; 1 Cor. 1:18–31). Following his teaching, Paul's churches would indeed go on to possess a diversity of membership which was without precedent within the Greek and Roman world.[4] Paul's communities were uniquely 'bridge-able'.

This I believe remains a huge challenge to the contemporary mainline Church: to be wholly 'bridge-able', and not defined by our own biases or culture. It is this quality, alongside ensuring that we regularly have ordinary and everyday contact with others, which will enable our congregations to become a spiritual home for those not currently members. In his bestselling memoir of 1950s parish life, *The Face of My Parish*, Tom Allan (whom we met in our last chapter as the Field Director of Tell Scotland) described a revolutionary approach to parish visitation, which would lead to 800 new members joining his congregation. However, over the following months, Allan watched in anguish as those same members began to drift away, a principal cause of which was the indifference and even hostility of the established congregation; often, it seemed, on the basis of social class.[5] A huge investment in making new connections is of no avail if a congregation has not learned to be 'bridge-able' and, as Paul and Bonhoeffer both discerned, a congregation can only be fully 'bridge-able' if its identity is rooted in Christ. Allan himself was to learn from these painful lessons, with his remarkable later ministry, in St George's Tron in the centre of Glasgow, marked by strong bonds within the congregation and an 'ever-open door' to all who were in the parish.[6]

The importance of our connections to all, regardless of official membership, was made real to Ricky Ross in one of the most moving moments he has experienced in a church gathering. As a child and teenager, he had grown up in the Brethren, with his adult spiritual journey bringing him into congregations in the Church of Scotland, the Scottish Episcopal Church, and latterly the Roman Catholic Church (Ricky would be quick to stress that such labels are not significant, for all are part of the universal Church). In his mother's later years, he once accompanied her to the evangelical church she attended on the south side of Glasgow. With this congregation having come from the Brethren tradition, Ricky presumed that he might not be allowed to participate in that morning's 'Breaking of the Bread', since during his childhood non-congregational members were only allowed to participate in this particular service if they possessed a letter of commendation from another Brethren fellowship. He had no such letter, but his mother categorically assured him that the table was open to 'all who loved the Lord'. It is difficult to overstate how much such moments matter.

Malcolm and Mavis Sargent were members of Didsbury Baptist Church in Manchester. Every Sunday morning, they had a set ritual: they would prepare a simple meal of soup, bread and fruit-loaf, in quantities sufficient to invite several visitors; following this, they would attend morning worship and, if any newcomers were present, Malcolm and Mavis would invite them for lunch. This they did on virtually every single Sunday for over twenty years. Even if visitors could not come on the first Sunday they were present, they knew they would be invited on their next visit, and if the church had no visitors then Malcolm and Mavis would invite any individual who would otherwise be eating their Sunday lunch alone.

Over the years, this practice helped transform the character and membership of their congregation and hospitality to outsiders became one of its defining charisms. In 2022, when Malcolm died, his funeral was packed, mourners having travelled hundreds of miles to be present, many having first got to know him through one of those Sunday lunches. Vibrant communities bridge and bond.

Healthy Community is Shaped by All Its Members

Sally and David Mann have ministered in London's East End, in the community of East Ham, for over thirty years. When Sally is asked why their ministry has lasted so long, when such community-based ministry becomes unsustainable in the long-term for so many who have attempted it, her response is instant: 'shared leadership'. When a leader is at the apex of a pyramid, she notes, with all decisions, responsibilities and pressures being channelled through them, the pressure eventually becomes intolerable. However, when leadership is shared, it acts more like a mesh, able to absorb across a wider area; and when one of the leaders is gone, perhaps only temporarily, the remaining leaders are able to absorb the pressures. Shared leadership is vital to healthy community.

In the churches of Cambuslang we had a problem. Our youth clubs were flourishing and, even though faith was important to their members, few of them wanted to come to church. An initial diagnosis was made: our worship was too traditional. Given that introducing a constant diet of contemporary Christian worship would be a step too far in either of our existing congregations, we decided to launch a new evening service. We ministers, alongside an older group of musicians, launched 'Church Unplugged'. The atmosphere was informal, the music contemporary and the teaching relevant. Our young people enthusiastically came along ... once.

Coaxing them to return required numerous phone calls, and the promise of a post-service trip to a burger restaurant. After several months, this did not feel as if it was working. People were coming for the fast-food, not for the worship. Something more was required than relevance and guitars, but precisely what it was, none of us adult leaders could discern.

About a year later, one of our young people, Amy, came to me with a proposal: could she and a group of other young people be 'given' our regular Sunday service, once every six weeks. Not an evening service, but the full-on proper morning service. She had even worked out a name for this venture: 'Stand Up for Sunday'. Inviting her peers to help plan, and with the help of a superbly gifted youth worker, the first 'Stand Up for Sunday' happened a few weeks later.

Surprisingly, the format of this new service looked more like a regular Sunday morning than Church Unplugged had ever done. There were prayers in pretty much all the usual places, we still sat in pews, we even had a reasonably formal bene-diction. Traditional hymns were mixed in with the new. The only real change to the format was that the sermon had been broken down into three smaller talks by the name of 'Bite-size Bible'. The whole thing grew and took on a life of its own. Whenever a young person got up to speak, or to lead an item, you could tell that they had seriously prepared. To be asked to present one of the three bite-size Bible slots was recognised as a serious badge of honour. Young people not only invited their friends but also their parents. Years after my own departure from Cambuslang, Stand Up for Sunday remained a regular part of congregational life.

What was the key difference between Stand Up for Sunday and Church Unplugged? Shared leadership. Our young people felt that Stand Up for Sunday was theirs. They invested in it. Not only them, but older congregational members intuitively understood that this was a good thing, and so smiled and sang through every service. For me it was a lesson that if we wished our community to grow in range and depth, there needed to be a widening of leadership; it couldn't all be through me, or even people who were like me. For a community to flourish, leader-ship must be shared.

Back to Paul

In this chapter we have outlined four essential principles of Christian community:

1 Community is a demanding task.
2 Community needs a demanding task.
3 Communities must bridge and bond.
4 Leadership must be shared.

Numbers 1, 3 and 4 are relatively easy to discern in the life of Paul's early Christian communities. But what of the second element, the demanding common task? This seems less readily apparent in the New Testament accounts. Paul's churches built no abbeys or tabernacles. What was their demanding common task? It seems that ultimately their task was both simple and utterly profound: to bear witness to the gospel. Against the pressures of persecution and prejudice, through the trials of internal conflict, they were to be communities of the Spirit and bearers of the Good News – the Good News that God in Christ is reconciling the world to God's self. That was their demanding coming task: be the gospel and bear the gospel. And despite all the pressures, despite all their fragility, this they did, across the ages, until that gospel eventually came to us. That is what Christian community can do.

12

Scripture

High up in the monastery tower of Wittenberg in Germany, a professor of theology is struggling to comprehend a verse in Paul's letter to the Romans. For Martin Luther, the meaning of this text is no abstract academic puzzle. Prone to great depression and following a narrow escape from a thunderstorm years before, he lives with a perpetual and terrifying fear of what will happen to his soul after death. His agonising derives from a particular word: 'righteousness'. According to Luther's most formative teachers, 'righteousness' was the right of God to punish sinners. Having no assurance that he might be spared such condemnation, Luther ponders desperately, night and day.

The problem for Luther was that if one were to primarily associate 'righteousness' with 'punishment', then Romans 1:18 made little sense. For here it was written that through the gospel, the Good News, God's righteousness had been revealed, and that the righteous person would live by faith. How could punishment, even righteous punishment, possibly be understood as good news? Then, at some point between 1515 and 1516, Luther experienced the revelation which would be a turning point. This turning point was not only in his life, but in the history of Western Europe: righteousness was not God's punishment but rather God's mercy, leading to the unmerited gift of grace, which 'clothes the sinner in God's own goodness'.[1]

In that moment, Luther's anxieties vanished; he felt as if he had been born for the second time, that he had entered through the 'open gates of paradise itself'.[2] Not only had this revelation changed his understanding of the gospel, but it further elevated his esteem for the scripture which had revealed this to him. Foundational to the Reformation, in which he would play a principal part, would be the doctrine of *Sola Scriptura*, which means Scripture Alone: no teaching or practice of the Church would be allowed unless it could also claim Biblical support. The scriptures would be the supreme authority by which the faithful would comprehend the Good News.

When challenged that the Bible was incomprehensible without the assistance of the Church's teaching, Luther claimed that, 'A simple layman armed with scripture is to be believed above a pope or council without it.'[3] With unimaginable industry, Luther not only led the most tumultuous change that the Church has probably ever experienced, but also translated the Old and New Testaments into German, a translation of such calibre that its influence continues to shape the German language today. Thanks to Luther's scholarship, and to the recently invented printing press, the ordinary people of the German lands were able to read or hear, without priestly intermediaries, the word of God for themselves.

For Luther, the scriptures give immediate access to God's own words. Not only are they the supreme means of divine instruction, they are also a primary means of divine presence. When one opens the book containing the Gospels, wrote Luther, and reads that 'Christ comes here or there, or how someone is brought to him', then, in faith, one should perceive that this is a moment when Christ himself 'is coming to us, or we are brought to him'.[4] Ultimately, we do not read the scriptures for information, but in order to encounter the one by whom they were inspired.

In the 1560s, as the Reformation reached Scotland, its esteem for the scriptures was not new to at least some of the Scots. To the north and west, among those known as the Celts or the Gaels, these had long been revered. The Bible was usually communicated orally, or its stories depicted on high stone crosses; and around the ninth century Celtic monks (probably on Iona) began work on the Book of Kells, a stunningly illuminated collection of Gospels and other exalted texts, and one of the great cultural achievements of the Middle Ages. Even further back, in the second century, a teacher from the Celtic or Gallic lands, Irenaeus of Lyon, had done more than perhaps any other to establish the Old and New Testaments as the Christian Canon. An affection for the scriptures had always run deep within the Celtic soul.

As in sixteenth-century Germany, or on ninth-century Iona, this affection for the Bible remains in Scotland, despite twenty-first-century Secularisation. When curious about the Christian faith, secular populations are as likely to read the Bible as they are to attend a local church and, in Scotland at least, the age group least likely to attend church (18–24-year-olds) are the most likely to read the Bible.[5] If, as we have previously suggested, the craving of the secular age is for divine encounter, it seems that, for many, reading the scriptures is how they seek to meet that hunger.

Though secular populations may retain a residual connection to the Bible, strikingly that affection has been much lost within the Church. In Scotland again, recent studies suggest that 230,000 non-churchgoers read the Bible on a regular basis, whereas 205,000 churchgoers do the same. In other words, being a regular Bible reader in Scotland actually means you are *less* likely to go to church. This is partly because the number of non-churchgoers who read the Bible is higher than we might expect, but also because the number of churchgoers who read the Bible is considerably lower, especially within the mainline.[6]

What has happened? How did a movement which grew from a rediscovery of scripture lose its affection for it? Protestant churches have indeed been defined by their reverence for scripture; in fact, this is so integral to their identity that an American President will brandish a Bible as a sign of his Christian credentials (and, by this, read Protestant Christian credentials). In addition, it is the Moderator of the Church of Scotland who presents the British monarch with a Bible at their coronation, proclaiming that this book contains 'the lively oracles of God'. The Bible may retain its importance as a Protestant symbol but, alas, among Protestant populations (and especially among mainline Protestants), it is rarely read. This is a phenomenon that goes back, as do so many of the patterns of mainline Protestantism, to the early days of the Reformation.

We previously noted the divide between the Magisterial

Reformation and the Radical Reformation which, as well as producing differing attitudes to the state, also produced differing practices in relation to the Bible.

Within the churches of the Radical Reformation, there was less concern for wider social conformity, and thus much greater receptivity towards individual Biblical interpretation.[7] It was in this part of the Reformation that personal scripture reading became more widespread.

Prominent in this, and famous for their repudiation of infant baptism, were the Anabaptists. In the German city of Münster they took *Sola Scriptura* to unforeseen extremes: their leader, John of Leiden, expelled the resident bishop, pronounced himself heir of David and King of the World, and sanctioned common ownership of property, polygamy and the smashing of images. This, however, was no blissful utopia but, with periodic episodes of violence, a reign of terror. Following a year-long siege, the city was recovered, John of Leiden barbarically executed, and the leaders of the Magisterial Reformation – Luther among them – vowed 'never again'.

The Anabaptists, however, persisted in their reading of the scriptures and protested against, as they saw it, the interpretative evasions of the Magisterial churches. They, and not the Magisterial Protestants, became known as a peculiarly Biblical people.[8] When persecuted and captured, as too frequently they were, their interrogators were stunned at the level of scriptural knowledge possessed by ordinary members. Such passion for the scriptures persisted down the centuries. Whenever an individual tells me today that as a young person they 'knew the Bible back to front', further conversation usually reveals that this was among the Brethren, the Baptists, or the Free Churches;[9] each of these being spiritual descendants of the Radical Reformation.

The Magisterial Reformers, however, aware of the lessons of Münster and other – as they saw it – Anabaptist excesses, were careful to ensure that individual liberty to read the scriptures was tempered by the teachings and authority of the Church. When the Reformation reached Scotland, its leader, John Knox, sought a school in every parish, not specifically to read the Bible, but rather the Shorter Catechism, in which scriptural teaching had already been selected and arranged to support the central tenets of Reformed theology.

Over the following centuries, it would be the churches of the Magisterial Reformation which, for the most part, would morph into the churches of the Protestant mainline. Scriptural reading was still encouraged, vernacular translations authorised (most famously, the King James Version of 1611).[10] But there remained a sense that individual judgement could not be wholly trusted, and instead it would be the suitably qualified, ministers and theological 'Doctors', who would ensure that interpretation sat within the boundaries of orthodox belief. Thus, ordinary mainline Protestants learned to devolve their interpretation of the scriptures to experts, and would, less frequently and less confidently, read the scriptures for themselves. Having less confidence in their own reading, and in particular what to do when the Bible got difficult, mainline Protestants became estranged from the scriptures. The Bible remained a symbol of identity, churches would give copies to their members when they were married or when their children were baptised, but these Bibles were rarely opened.

A rediscovery of the Bible has been at the heart of every renewal the Protestant Church has known. How might we mainliners reclaim our affection for the scriptures? Here are four essential moves.

Learning to Read by Ourselves

As we have already noted, mainline Protestants have been taught, however subtly, that their own readings of scripture are liable to be suspect, and that scriptural interpretation should be devolved to trained preachers and scholars. How might this be undone? Here we might draw on practices which derive from within the Catholic monastic tradition, but which were also endorsed by the early Reformers (however much they were later forgotten). Many of these build on the insight of the second-century teacher Origen, who believed that the reading of scripture can become a 'sacrament' – an activity in which God is especially present. Thus, the purpose of scripture reading is no longer to recover the one absolute and apparent meaning of the text (and woe betide the one who arrives at an incorrect answer), but instead to be immersed in a new and different world – a world in which we may be reassured, or inspired, or puzzled or intrigued.

Historic methods of reading scripture which build on Origen's insights include *Lectio Divina* (meaning 'divine reading') and Ignatian meditation. In these, the scriptures are read or listened to repeatedly, prayerfully and slowly. Participants are encouraged to notice how the text speaks to their intuition, intellect, emotions and imagination. Instantaneous agreement may not be our first response when engaging with the scriptures in this way. Instead, we may feel shock, surprise, affirmation, hope, confusion, indifference, curiosity, revulsion or delight. It is not that any of these responses is either 'right' or 'wrong', but rather, that they are indisputably 'there', and in all of these we listen for the voice of God.

In learning not to suppress our authentic response to scripture, nor being cowed by the knowledge of experts, we are learning to encounter God in scripture and also paying attention to the self. Given that divine encounter and the turn to the self are two essential elements of church renewal in the secular age, it is not difficult to identify reasons for the popularity of these approaches in recent years. Such approaches have become a mainstay of retreats, small groups and also podcasts and apps.

Mary, the mother of Jesus, is one of the great heroes of this kind of scriptural reading. Knowing how to ponder, treasure – and also when to be perplexed (Luke 1:29; 2:19) – Mary's scriptural engagement is transformed into song. As she sings 'My soul magnifies the Lord' (Luke 2:46–56) she blends several Biblical passages, most of all the song of another mother, Hannah (1 Sam. 2:1–10). Augmenting and improvising, Mary poetically weaves sacred text around a celebration of justice and her own personal story. Authentically and imaginatively engaging with the Bible, her life, her passions and her emotions, Mary teaches us how to read the scripture for ourselves.

Learning to Read Together

Two of the great saints of the Church in Scotland were Margaret and Ian Fraser. Here, 'Church' is used in the widest sense, for though rooted in the Church of Scotland Margaret and Ian lived and worshipped alongside Christians of all denominations, and alongside many on the fringe. Their great passion was the study of 'Small Christian Communities' or 'Base Christian Communities'. Travelling around Europe, South-East Asia, Central and South America, they would sleep on floors, eat in the poorest of homes, and listen to the songs and stories of the people. Frequently these communities sat on the edge of institutional church life; some of the communities had been deemed suspect by the ecclesiastical authorities, others had even been banned. Despite – or even because of – their distance from the Church as an institution, these communities shone in their worship, their sense of community and their work for justice. Frequently, at the heart of each community's life, Margaret and Ian noted, was the communal study of the Bible. It was in the Bible that people understood God's passion for justice and were challenged to recognise their own gifts and potential. Frequently it was the Bible which expanded their vision of what they might become, and of how God's will might be done on earth as in heaven.[11]

'The Gospel in Solentiname' is one of the most celebrated collections of such scriptural studies. From 1965 to 1977, on the Solentiname archipelago of Lake Nicaragua, a Catholic priest, Ernesto Cardenal, would gather his parishioners during the Sunday Mass to study that week's Gospel passage, verse by verse. Copies of the text would be passed around, and for the benefit of those who were illiterate he would ask one of the best readers (usually a young person) to read the passage. Then, instead of a sermon, a discussion would take place. Each would bring their own perspectives: Marcelino was mystic, his wife Rebeca always spoke about love, Olivia was theological, Elvis dreamed of the perfect society of the future. The oppression of Nicaragua's then dictatorship, and the struggle for liberation, were never far from their conversation. During the course of these Bible studies, three of the community's members would be killed.

Reading the transcripts of these conversations,[12] the affinity felt by the campesinos of Nicaragua for the peasants of first-century Galilee, with both groups living under military oppression, is immediately apparent. Insights, which more affluent commentators would miss, abound. In one of their longest discussions, on the parable of the talents (Matt. 25:14–30), a Colombian poet called William begins by pronouncing that this is a 'lousy parable'; he says this because he knows the kind of ruthless speculators who invest sums as vast as these, and surely Jesus could not possibly be commending such individuals? The congregation then remembers wealthy individuals whom they know, who invest in banks and do not share ('and look, there's a bank there!' says William of verse 27). Surely Jesus is not commending the greedy? Rather, they wonder, is he exposing the exploitative economics of his day? Then a consensus emerges that the investments Jesus commends are absolutely not of money, because for money to grow like the investments in the parable is 'not natural'. Instead, this is about sharing hens, and corn and kidney beans, and above all it is about sharing love. Love is the commodity which is meant for the kind of growth the parable describes.

Ernesto Cardenal did not record his congregation's earliest conversations; consequently, the published transcripts all belong to a later period, when there is an obvious confidence and sophistication in people's voices. This feels like something which the community has learned: how to imagine, to listen and to argue. Cardenal's own contributions usually offer an insight from a commentary or a theologian. However, these are never suffocating, but instead, with a light touch, facilitate further conversation.

Reading in community teaches us that Biblical study is always a conversation: a conversation with God, a conversation with our neighbour, a conversation with the world of politics, psychology or history; and sometimes it is a conversation between different parts of the Bible itself. Such conversation is not a threat, or a means of weakening the text. Rather, conversation in Solentiname was a means through which the text spoke with a power which would not have been present if those taking part had only studied the text alone.

Earlier we noted that mainline Protestants often draw back from the Bible when it gets difficult: because of apparent conflicts with science, contemporary morality, or because the meaning seems unclear. In communal study, judicious scholarship and discussion begin to loosen these problems. And if the text remains obscure, the community shares the burden of its impenetrability, until, it is hoped, some kind of light might emerge.

Learning to Read Symbolically

In 1871, the Princeton theologian Charles Hodge published the first volume of his *Systematic Theology*, stating that just as it was the task of scientists to arrange and systematise the facts of the natural world, so it was the task of theologians to arrange and systematise the 'facts of the Bible'. Thus, for Hodge and his followers, the Bible was to be regarded as a repository of historically accurate data, and any attempt to downplay this historicity was to undermine the very authority of the scripture itself.[13] The doctrine of Biblical inerrancy – meaning that the Bible is factually correct in every idea and detail – had begun to assert itself.

It is important to comprehend just how utterly new such claims were. Up until then, the Church had never made such assertions so strongly. Apparent contradictions in the scripture, such as differing accounts of the death of Judas, were known to the early Church, but attempts to resolve these were neither persuasive nor thought to be particularly necessary.[14] When a Syrian scholar by the name of Tatian had once offered to the Church his Diatesseron, a combined harmony of the four Gospels, Irenaeus had argued that the Church should reject any such synopsis: just as the world needed four winds, the North, the South, the East and the West, so too the Church required four Gospels.[15] Not for the first or last time, the Church chose diversity, despite its challenges, over manufactured uniformity.

Even when earlier scholars had employed the term 'literal' what was intended was a plain interpretation, not the strident historicity demanded by Hodge and his followers. For writers such as Augustine of Hippo, some passages were clearly intended for figurative interpretation; to insist on a literal reading was a 'miserable slavery of the soul'.[16] Furthermore, Augustine denounced 'reckless and incompetent expounders of scripture'[17] whose interpretations clearly violated our knowledge of the natural world.

For Augustine, attempts to resolve Biblical inconsistencies through interpretative gymnastics were also unnecessary: the Bible was a human as well as a divine text and, as such, would always be in some sense 'finite'. Its very limitations were directing us towards the perfection of Christ which was, for Augustine, scripture's primary purpose.[18]

For Augustine and many others, the apparent inconsistencies of the scriptures were not the problem that later, more literal interpreters imagined them to be. And neither were symbolic interpretations some desperate attempt to evade the difficulties of the text, but often the preferred and most powerful form of interpretation.

The power of Genesis, for example, is not in arguing that the world was created in a week, but in celebrating the universe as intentionally good and that all people are bearers of the divine image. Jonah's three-day entombment in the whale was, for Jesus, above all a symbol of his own impending death and resurrection (Matt. 12:39–40). For Paul, Old Testament passages about muzzling oxen were categorically not about livestock, but about a pastor's right to be paid (Deut. 25:4 and 1 Cor. 9:9).

Symbolic reading is an invitation to the imagination: to view, for example, the Exodus narrative as God's triumph over the gods of empire, David's defeat of Goliath as an encouragement for the young to refuse the weaponry of the old, and Peter's walking on water as an invitation to step out of safety and enjoy Jesus' company in the middle of chaos. Above all, these symbolic readings often lead us into what are sometimes called 'Christological' readings of the scripture, which many regard as the most important readings. There are places where we discern the presence of Christ in older passages such as the psalms ('The

Lord's my shepherd', Ps. 23); the almost-sacrifice of Isaac in Genesis 22 (long seen as an allegory of the crucifixion); and the many passages in the prophets which, as well as being related to their own time, also point forward to the life of Jesus (most famously, Isaiah 53).

To adopt a symbolic reading is not to deny the historic veracity of the scriptures. It would be hard to argue that, for the New Testament writers, the reality of Jesus' resurrection did not matter. Their accounts have a compelling credibility: the counter-cultural reliance on the testimony of women, the willingness to offer detail, the almost casual way that Paul refers to the many living witnesses (1 Cor. 15:6). Even the relatively minor contradictions, like eyewitness testimony after a major event, suggest we are dealing with reality rather than conspiracy. However, symbol also matters hugely: in the writings of Paul, for example, the resurrection is both a historic event and an essential symbol of life's continuing power over death.

There are many such passages where symbolic and historic readings sit together. There are also some where a symbolic reading is not only legitimate but, as Augustine recognised, to be preferred. We should not allow any recent insistence on 'inerrancy' to suggest that this undermines the authority of the scripture. Instead, the Spirit leads us, through different forms of interpretation, into the truth which sets us free.

Learning to Read with Compassion

Jesus is being set a trap. In the synagogue, on the Sabbath, there is a man with a withered hand. With all eyes upon him, especially the accusatory eyes of the Pharisees, Jesus is asked a question: 'Is it lawful to cure on the sabbath?' (Matt. 12:10).

How does he address this challenge? On one side is the literal interpretation of law with its Sabbath prohibitions, and on the other side is love. There might even be some escape routes ('come back tomorrow' or 'healing isn't real work') but for Jesus there is little hesitation. Reminding his opponents that God desires 'mercy not sacrifice', Jesus turns to the man and says, 'Stretch out your hand!' He has chosen love. Always, always, always, Jesus will choose love. Without equivocation, without reserve, without caution, Jesus will always choose love. When interpreting the scriptures, even if this apparently means setting aside the scripture to be true to scripture, Jesus will always choose love.

Echoing Paul's words in 1 Corinthians 13 – that even the most noble actions are worthless if done without love – Augustine would later reassert this primacy of love when reading the scripture:

> Whoever, therefore thinks that he understands the divine scriptures or any part of them so that it does not build the double love of God and neighbour does not understand it at all.[19]

Remarkably, Augustine went on to add that any reading that built up love was truthful, even a reading not intended by the original author.

It is this criterion of love which must be applied to all our reading of scripture, including its most troubling parts. If our reading of Ephesians 6:5, that slaves obey their earthly masters, suggests that the owning of slaves is legitimate, then we must read again, for such a reading does not conform to love. If our reading of 1 Samuel 15:3, that Saul slaughters the Amalekites, leads us to believe that ethnic genocide is ever legitimate, then we must read again, for such a reading does not conform to love. If the only reading we can find is that a certain passage is a record of what people once sincerely believed God had told them to do, then perhaps that is the closest reading that comes to love. Love does not give us the easiest reading of scripture, nor is the meaning of love always clear, but still it remains the criterion by which we read, for any reading of scripture which does not love cannot be of God.

For those who grew up in environments where scripture was interpreted with a fierce toxicity, used to justify violence against children or women, used to bolster the narcissistic tendencies of a bully, or used to control sexuality in ways which saw our bodies as an enemy, then might the path away from such readings be this: the criterion of love. And if the memory of how scripture was used is, for us, traumatic, then perhaps, for a season (and I write this advisedly), the scripture might not be read and we might simply concentrate on bringing to mind the one to whom scripture points, the one who taught us to love.

How We Read

Several studies have identified that one of the greatest hindrances to scripture reading is its traditional format, the perplexing arrangement (to the uninitiated) of columns, chapters and verse. This is a reminder that the original scriptures had none of these things. Just as chapters and verses were introduced because 'they worked', so we might also experiment with the order of books, the formatting of pages, removal of chapter and verse indicators, to find what works. The text of the scripture is canonical; none of these other additions are. There are valid arguments for a literal translation (like the New Revised Standard Version used in this book) or for free translation (like the New Living Translation, or *The Message*); once again, we should use what best enables the scriptures to speak to us, we should use what works.[20]

In this chapter we have often cited Augustine of Hippo, one of the greatest teachers of the early Church. His whole journey into scripture and into faith was transformed when he heard a child in a neighbour's garden repeatedly singing 'Take up and read, take up and read'. In whatever way that works, the song remains good today: 'Take up and read. Take up and read'.

13

Justice

At the Greenbelt Christian Arts Festival of 2023, hundreds of
people packed into an overflowing tent to hear the son of a
Church of Scotland minister speak on 'a country where poverty
does not exist'. This son of the manse began by describing the
destitution he had witnessed growing up in 1950s Scotland: he
recalled the horrors of Victorian-era housing, floods destroy-
ing people's homes, members of his class at school in obvious
and desperate poverty, and the loss of jobs when factories had
closed down. But now, he said, the poverty being seen in the
United Kingdom today was of a severity he had never expected
to see again in his lifetime: children going to school hungry,
families choosing between heating and eating, people queuing
at foodbanks after a backbreaking day's work. He listed statistics: 400,000 families who don't have a cooker (and, because
of that, no regular hot food); 700,000 sleeping on the floor
because they can't afford a bed; 6 million families who don't
have chairs or a table in the kitchen; 14 million people officially registered as poor; 19 million people who don't have the
resources that every family should have to lead a decent life.

As the former Prime Minister Gordon Brown spoke, his
voice quivering with barely controlled fury, the audience was
shocked at the reality he was describing, and many, those living
and working in the United Kingdom's poorest communities,
were also grateful that he was naming a reality which they
knew only too well. Listening to Gordon Brown, I was struck
that here was a man who could have lost touch through many
years spent working in privileged and rarefied company, who
had endured countless personal attacks and had every excuse
to step back, who could have allowed cynicism to temper the

passion of his youth; but no, the fire still remained, the passion for justice was undimmed and the values which he had learned in a Church of Scotland manse had clearly gone deep.

A passion for justice lies deep within the mainline soul.

But tragically, there is also another story.

On the outside of the small church near Edinburgh in which I was baptised, a set of stone steps leads to an upstairs door and into the 'miners' gallery'. I vividly remember the day that my dad, his eyes moist with sadness and fury, told me the story of its construction. Miners from the nearby colliery had wanted to come to church but had been refused entry because the wealthy did not wish their experience of worship to be ruined by the uncomfortable proximity of unkempt, poor and, to their mind, stinking miners. And so, these miners and their families, poor as they were, had found the money and labour to build a gallery with outside steps so that at no point would they come into contact with their more affluent neighbours – individuals who wanted to worship without their noses or their eyes being offended by the presence of the poor.

This is the darker side of my own denomination; although we have often broken down the barriers of injustice, too often we have also sought to preserve them. There have, alas, always been two strands to the politics of the mainline Church: the radical and the reactionary.

In 1788 the Church of Scotland's General Assembly received no fewer than three petitions which called for the abolition of slavery; but despite offering sympathetic words, the Assembly decided (out of anxiety not to offend the King) to take no further concrete action. During the nineteenth-century clearances of Scottish Estates, when subsistence farmers were evicted to make way for sheep, there were some Presbyterian ministers who railed against greed and oppression, but many others adjured their members to accept this injustice as God's good and perfect will. There have always been two strands.

We shall return to the second strand shortly, but first we must ask, 'What is the first strand of radical political engagement?' What is this passion for justice, learned by Gordon Brown in his childhood manse in Kirkcaldy; this passion for justice which

runs not just through the mainline, but through the whole of
the Christian Church?

Justice Loves Where Pain is Greatest

Recalling his upbringing, Gordon Brown spoke of the many
individuals who came to the door of his parents' home when
they were desperate or hungry or felt like they had been 'thrown
on to the scrapheap' after losing their jobs.[1] This sounds not
very different from a house in Capernaum in Galilee where the
crowds gathered, even breaking the roof (Jesus' own roof it
would appear) to ensure contact between the healer and those
whose need was greatest (Mark 1:32–34; 2:1–12).

The Peruvian theologian Gustavo Gutiérrez described this
divine passion for those whose need is greatest as God's *opción
preferencial*.[2] When translated into English as 'God's preferential option for the poor', this can be wrongly understood as
an assertion that God prefers poor people to wealthy people.
This is the opposite of Gutiérrez's meaning. Rather, from the
conviction that God loves all universally, love moves first to
the place of greatest unlove, in order that all may be loved; to
the place where life is under greatest threat, in order that all
might live; to where poverty is greatest, so that all can share
in the abundance of God. In the mainline, this means that our
mission begins with the poorest; and this is never an afterthought.

The preferential option means that in Sally Mann's church in
East Ham, new Christians learn discipleship through working
for justice. Thus, justice is not an activity in which someone
may become involved after all the other basics are covered. The
preferential option meant that at the beginning of the second
week of the Glasgow University Mission of 1994 the speaker
who had been asked to speak on 'God's passion for justice' spent
his address castigating the organising committee (of which I was
a member) for not having invited him to speak at the beginning
of week one. The preferential option means that I do not sort
out all my emails from various committees, ensure the most

powerful people in our structures are being looked after, and all the tasks which make me look good are done, before getting round to possibly visiting the poorest people in our parish; nor does it mean that God's passion for justice gets an occasional mention in special services. The preferential option means we always begin at that crowded door in Capernaum, at the place where the need is greatest.

Justice Protests against Unjust Structures

For Gutiérrez, the option for the poor has a second dimension. It means standing on the side of the poor in their struggle for justice, a side which God, in Christ, has already taken.[3] It means tackling the structures of injustice, as well as alleviating the pain which injustice has caused.

Sally Foster-Fulton, Head of Christian Aid Scotland and Moderator of the Church of Scotland for 2023–24, speaks of her own journey as an activist. Growing up in North Carolina, she witnessed injustice in her hometown, of situations to which she would cry out: 'That's not fair!' From that initial passion she began to discern that injustice cannot, ultimately, be overcome through individual acts of charity, but through understanding the policies, patterns and structures which make people poor. 'It's like the layers of an onion,' she says, 'you keep peeling back and discovering that there is more there.'

We might object that this struggle against the structures of injustice sounds more like a leftist (and even Marxist) obsession, rather than an authentically Christian vocation. A re-reading of the Gospels reveals otherwise. Frequently, the scriptures, from the Jewish law to the prophets, from the Gospels to the book of Revelation, condemn the patterns and practices of injustice. They taught that land had to be returned on the fiftieth year, and debts forgiven (Lev. 25:1–55). They castigated those who had forgotten about injustice but still attended religious festivals (Amos 5:21–24). In overturning the tables of the temple, Jesus taught us to confront any institution which robs the poorest, regardless of its religious credentials (Mark 11:15–19). And the book of Revelation depicts in the starkest terms the structures of empire which corner the market, perpetuate injustice and commodify human lives (Rev. 13:17; 18:9–13). In the Bible, so much more often than we perceive with our more affluent eyes, the text condemns any structure which makes the poorest poorer and allows the wealthiest to reap the rewards.

Justice Tells Stories

One of the structures which continually works against the poorest people is the conventional narrative of our media. In short, we tend to be far more curious about the lives of the wealthy than those of the poor. And when we do tell stories of those in poverty, these are often focused on 'benefit cheats' or 'bogus asylum seekers'. In a 2016 report, 'The Lies We Tell Ourselves', a group of UK churches exposed six perennial myths about those experiencing poverty: that 'they' are lazy, addicted to drink, poor at budgeting, 'on the fiddle', have an easy life, and were the cause of the UK government's deficit. Each of these myths is utterly false.[4]

To falsely accuse the poorest of being the cause of their own poverty is not a new phenomenon. The founder of Methodism, John Wesley, wrote in 1753: 'So wickedly devilishly false is that common objection "they are poor, only because they are idle".' To suppress the truth about poverty, the causes of poverty, and above all the stories of people who experience poverty, is not merely a crime of misinformation, it can lead to the worst of consequences.

In June 2017, the Grenfell Tower, a twenty-four-storey block of flats in west London, was engulfed in a catastrophic fire. Seventy-four of its residents died; many more suffered horrendous, life-changing injuries. However, this deadly blaze was, tragically, no surprise to those who lived there. For years, its residents had been campaigning for improved fire-safety. The local council's response had not been to improve the safety of the tower but to threaten several of its residents with legal action. Two of those threatened, Mariem Elgwahry and Nadia

Choucair, were among those who would later be killed in the blaze.

Reflecting on this tragedy, Channel 4 journalist Jon Snow wrote that he and the rest of the media were culpable because, habitually, they did not tell the stories of those who are poorest; that poor people were deemed 'not particularly interesting' by media organisations, and so, since their stories were untold, wider society found it easier not to care.[5]

In contrast to the news agenda of contemporary western societies, Jesus was always telling stories about the poorest people; and not as an outsider, for he was a poor man himself. He told stories about servants who lived under mountains of debt; victims of violence; widows whose savings had gone missing; individuals about to lose their jobs; rich men whose luck had turned; farmhands on the ancient equivalent of zero-hours contracts; and those who lived on the streets. In his parable of the rich man and the beggar, it was the rich man who remained anonymous, and the poor man, Lazarus, who was given his name.

To tell the story of those who live with poverty is the work of the Poverty Truth Commission. It is a remarkable organisation, formed in Scotland in 2009 with support from, among others, the mainline Church. Modelled on the Truth and Reconciliation Commission of South Africa, the Poverty Truth Commission's aim is to enable Scotland's poorest people to tell their own story. The purpose of this is not to generate sympathy nor to make the poorest people appear as idealised saints, but to influence decision-making. Enabling the poorest to tell their own story leads to better policies, better relationships, and the sharing of power. This does not sound very different from the kingdom of Jesus: the poor man who told stories about the poor.

Justice is about Being Friends

In order to reclaim its gift for justice, the mainline Church must better become a community where the affluent and poor not only sit together, but also lead together. Too often, perhaps, the mainline Church has become an affluent Church and less like the church in Corinth, the majority of whose members Paul described as weak, foolish and despised. My friend Martin, whose lifelong calling has been to live with the poorest and to call the Church to do the same, does not actually like the word 'poor'. He prefers to speak of people who are 'struggling against poverty'. For him, 'poor' is a label which hides all that is particular and human about an individual person.

When I told Martin the story of my father's first congregation and the wealthy not wanting 'smelly miners' to sit with them in the body of the Kirk, he remembered a contrasting story from the most rarefied church setting of them all. Martin had once been invited, alongside leaders of community groups from all around the world, to meet with Pope Francis in the Vatican. Many of those present were wearing their smartest clothes and yet, recalls Martin, these were still t-shirts and jeans with holes in them. This attire was in stark contrast to that of the Vatican officials in their dinner suits and bow ties. The Pope spent two to three hours in conversation with this group of activists, and at the end said something which might be considered highly offensive in another setting: that it had been 'great to be in the company of people who smelled like the poor'.[6] Pope Francis has learned something, which Jesus had always known: that to be around those who are poorest is to be at home.[7]

At the end of his parable of the dishonest manager, Jesus makes the perplexing statement that his disciples should 'make friends for yourselves by means of dishonest wealth so that when it is gone, they may welcome you into the eternal homes' (Luke 16:9). Jesus' instruction seems almost mercenary or unworthy, which is perhaps why it is rarely commented on, but he seems to be suggesting that if we who are wealthy make friends with the poorest, then it is the poorest who will first welcome us into the kingdom. This can only happen if our churches are places where the wealthiest and the poorest both sit and lead together.

Justice (and the Gospel) is Taught by the Poorest

In being a Church of the poorest, with the poorest and for the poorest, we make one further essential discovery: the poorest people teach the rest of us the gospel. On Christmas Eve 1994, I was invited to a congregation of some of India's poorest people, the Dalits. It was a night I will never forget. When I arrived, I felt a sense of embarrassment at my wealth and privilege, but this did not seem to register with those who were my hosts. I was welcomed simply because I was another human being. These people seemed to smile from their very soul, they sang Christmas carols, some Indian and some western ones, with unrestrained conviction. It feels such a cliché to say it, but that night it was they who were rich. And at the end of the evening, I was told that these people, whom I had never previously met, had a gift for me. They had bought me a Bible in the local language, Malayalam. They weren't to know that for some time I had been wanting a local Bible but hadn't had enough money to afford one. They, the poorest of people, had given me, the rich man, the perfect gift. I still have it, Sathyaveda Pustakam, the Malayalam Bible. I discovered something that night about Christmas. I think the reason that Jesus was born among the poorest was because God knew that they would look after him.

That night, when the poorest people literally gave me the gospel, they also taught me the gospel. It is the poorest who teach us the scriptures. This is what Ernesto Cardenal discovered when reading the Bible in Solentiname. He observed that the 'commentaries of the campesinos are usually of greater profundity than that of many theologians, but of a simplicity like that of the gospel itself. That is not surprising. The gospel was written for them, by people like them.'[8] Ian Fraser, after visiting the Philippines in 1982, noted that the world of the Gospels, with 'the oppression of landlords, the tough business of finding and netting fish, the lighting and cleaning of houses, the baking of bread',[9] was well-known to the poor.

Why is it, when wealthier Christians choose to live in poorer areas, they will often comment: 'The people here have taught me how to be a Christian, for God was with them, long before I arrived'? Why is this? Is it because the poorest have seen something to which the rich are blind – that though the world too often works against them, they have known the unrelenting solidarity of God? Is it because they have come to know that what truly matters is living itself? That they have learned an honesty not known to the wealthy, with our carefully curated and perfected lives? Is it because the poorest have spotted grace and cling to it, whereas we who are wealthy still secretly believe that it is our achievements which earn our place in the kingdom? It is vital not to romanticise poverty, and yet I have often discovered all of these things to be true. It is the poor who teach us the gospel.

The Opposite of Justice

At the beginning of this chapter, we observed that the mainline Church has often exhibited two different strands of political engagement: the radical and the reactionary. We are called to the radical, but when we get frightened we let the reactionary take over. In today's mainline Church, with mounting pressure on resources, there is a pressure to rein in our radical strand, to first ensure our survival before we attend to the struggle for justice. This, however, is a temptation we must resist. To rein back the radical strand is not a temporary and neutral move; instead, it allows the reactionary to take over and we start asking miners to build outside staircases.

As we have already noted, Old Testament theologian Walter Brueggemann has termed this reactionary move the 'economics of scarcity', the retrenchment we undergo when we fear we no longer have enough. Resisting the pressures of scarcity means trusting instead in 'manna economics' (Exod. 16:1–36), of trusting in the God who gives bread in the desert, and who always gives enough.[10]

In his second letter to the Corinthians, Paul cites the remarkable example of his churches who, despite experiencing extreme poverty, joyfully donated to the Jerusalem Church. For him, such generosity depends on a key principle of manna economics: that we always share our wealth, that 'the one who had much did not have too much, and the one who had little did not have too little' (2 Cor. 8:15, quoting Exod. 16:18). If we are not either generously sharing, or being generously shared with, then something is wrong.

Though we might fear decline and scarcity, just about all mainline churches remain places of abundance. With those who experience the suffocating forces of poverty we are called to share our wealth, to stand with all in the quest for justice, and to discover that it is the poorest who will teach us the gospel. In our increasingly divided world, where vicious poverty has returned to even the most affluent societies, the need has never been more urgent.

14

Land

The great missiologist Lesslie Newbigin once noted that in the New Testament the Church is known by two kinds of relationship. Either it is known in relation to God in Christ, or it is known in relation to a place: 'the Church of God that is in Corinth', 'the Churches of Galatia', 'the Church of the Thessalonians', 'the Church in Philadelphia'. Similarly, the Church's members are also identified by place: 'the saints in the region of Achaia', 'the saints who are in Ephesus', 'to all the saints in Christ Jesus who are in Philippi'. Place is core to our identity as churches and as saints.

Today, this sense of place remains strong within the churches of the mainline. The formal relationship varies. Some denominations enjoy a strong affinity with their local communities, despite there being no constitutionally defined relationship; while others sit within a legally defined network of parishes. Within the Church of Scotland, much recent debate has been directed towards this relationship with place. Enshrined within our 'Third Article Declaratory' is a 'distinctive call and duty to bring the ordinances of religion to the people in every parish of Scotland'. For many, this is a preposterous claim, a grandiose relic of Christendom. In a secular society, the idea of any religious organisation making claim on the territory of the land is an insult to millions of non-religious Scots. And yet, in 2010, a commission tasked with reviewing the Third Article concluded that it was still required, not least because civic institutions and leaders still valued and expected it.[1]

On the night of my ordination, in Flemington Hallside Church on the edge of Glasgow, I had a particularly heightened sense of this call to place. Present in the congregation alongside regular churchgoers were teachers, councillors and community organisers. Though these individuals were not regular church-goers, the local church still mattered to them. At the end of the evening, I was given a large brown envelope by our Presbytery Clerk. It contained three items: a letter of welcome, contact details for a counselling service, and a map of the parish. I often looked at the map over the following years, not to find a par-ticular street or farm, but simply to sense again this calling to parish and to place. Throughout the remainder of this chapter, we will explore five dimensions of this calling to place: atten-tiveness, lostness, hereness, darkness and connectedness.

Attentiveness

Nan Shepherd was a Scottish teacher and writer who immersed herself in the life, form and presence of the Cairngorm Moun-tains. In her classic work, *The Living Mountain*, she writes of a quest which brought her outwards, into the mountains, and inwards, into the soul. In the footsteps of John Muir, she discov-ered that 'going out ... was really going in'.[2] During her many hours in the mountains, Shepherd was continually entranced. The more she looked, the more she saw; the more she listened, the more she heard.

The nature writer Robert Macfarlane gives this continued work of attention a surprising description: he calls it 'parochial', the work of the parish.[3] Here, 'parochial' does not mean narrow or insular. Rather, it is the poetic task of seeing universal truth in particular details. The Irish poet Patrick Kavanagh once wrote:

> To know fully, even one field or one land is a lifetime's experience. In the world of poetic experience it is depth that counts, not width. A gap in a hedge, a smooth rock surfacing a narrow lane, a view of a woody meadow, the stream at the junction of four small fields – these are as much as man can fully experience.[4]

When the parish is noticed – gently, humbly and sincerely; with a discipline that takes in the broad sweep and the tiniest detail – then the Church is made more ready for mission. The parish also notices that it is being noticed, and it too becomes curious.

It is tempting to say that the Church should engage with parish without concern for itself, purely altruistically, without any hint of self-interest. This, however, is disingenuous. The mainline needs its parish. Without this sacred land, a congregation would lose an essential part of itself; it would become disembodied and adrift.

Lostness

For all of its importance to mainline identity, this journey into neighbourhood, if done properly, will also include – and probably begin with – the disconcerting experience of being lost. In his account of parish life, *The Face of My Parish*, Tom Allan recounted the beginnings of his ministry in Glasgow's North Kelvinside. This involved an exercise which was radically innovative for its day; he invited a team of theological students (backed by a small number of his more intrepid parishioners) to survey the homes of his parish. When the results came back, Allan was devastated to discover that only 60 per cent of the homes in his parish had a church connection. Such a level of disconnection, he wrote, 'shattered any remnants of complacency which were in me'. How much greater is our dislocation today? After a prayer walk round her local parish, as part of a course on local mission in 2021, my friend Lynn reached a similar verdict to that of Tom Allan seventy years earlier: 'I realised how irrelevant we are,' she concluded.

Yet this lostness, this sense of irrelevance, is essential to the experience of finding our sense of place. Ten years ago, a one-day mission conference was held in one of my current congregations. At lunchtime, the invited speaker went on to the street outside and asked every passer-by what they knew of their parish church. Almost every respondent said they knew very little. When this was reported back to the conference's post-lunch session, the congregation were stunned – but after shock came a resolve to act. Further community research led to an anti-poverty project and also brought a renewed attention to the congregation's youth project; both of these projects remain in place today and have had a huge influence on many within the area. I do wonder how many times we will have to become lost again, as we seek to address the new challenges which the future will bring.

In scripture, the place of being lost is sometimes called 'wilderness'. It would seem that nearly always we must go there prior to our greatest calling: the Israelites must wander the desert before entering the promised land; Jesus will spend forty days in the desert prior to the rest of his ministry; and after his conversion Paul will head to Arabia for several years. In order to be found, we must first be lost. In the words of David Wagoner's famous poem, 'lost' becomes a 'powerful stranger' who introduces us to the place called 'here'.[5]

Hereness

United Methodist Church minister Lydia Sohn says of the Southern California community in which she is pastor 'Clare-mont is my land.' Conscious of her own childhood, which was characterised by frequent moves until her parents purchased the home in which they still live, Lydia argues that we need to reclaim a 'theology of stability'. To be stable is to embrace 'here' and resist the illusory temptations of 'somewhere else'. This is not a commitment to being static or unchanged, but rather it is to grow as a tree grows, rooted in one place but still growing. It is an appetite to discover the strange within the already familiar. As the Irish poet John O'Donohue once wrote, 'It is strange to be here. The mystery never leaves you.'[6]

The question may be asked, 'What of heaven? Surely that is another place for which we should yearn? Do not we sojourn as strangers in an alien land?' (Heb. 11:13). There is indeed a sense in which we should always be 'living in tents', mobile and not besotted with the idolatry of place. Places are holy, but they are not gods. However, as one of my early teachers, a geographer by the name of David Livingstone, used to remind our congregation in Belfast, the scripture does not teach that we ultimately ascend to a disembodied paradise, but rather that heaven is 'coming down' (Rev. 21:2).[7] In an inspiring sermon he once proclaimed: 'The Grand Canyon will be there, Belfast Lough will be there, the Holy Lands will be there.'[8] To yearn for heaven is not to yearn for evacuation, but rather to yearn that the kingdom come on earth, that our parish be redeemed.

Darkness

Some of the most disturbing characters in the Gospels are the demons. We can attempt to explain these away, as pre-modern attempts at understanding mental illness, but this does not do justice to the Gospel accounts. Why do the demons need to be silenced? How do they know who Jesus is? And why, if this is simply a pre-modern delusion, are there so few demons in the even more pre-modern Old Testament? What is going on?

The Gospels testify to malevolent powers, which perhaps become all the more visible (or rather audible) when the one who is wholly benevolent is present. Perhaps the demons are the unhealthiness of religious power, or the violence of imperial power, carried within the bodies of the Gospels' Galilean population. There is an inexplicable darkness present within the world of the Gospels.

Sometimes in the parish today, as in the Gospels, this darkness is manifestly demonic. One of my mentors, one of the most sensible and rational people I know, was for many years his presbytery's exorcist. He knew of the dark powers that could haunt a person or a home. He also knew of the prayers that brought light where previously darkness had reigned.

Such talk was less strange to Celtic ears. The ancient prayers of the Gaels frequently sought protection from hostile powers. George MacLeod, a modern-day Celt, spoke of a dark and 'smothering malevolence' he once encountered, early one morning in Iona Abbey. Alastair McIntosh, on his pilgrimage along the coast of Harris and Lewis, also spoke of the need to ward off dark powers.[9] Such talk would have been understood by a board member in my first congregation: posted to Germany not long after the Second World War, he remembered the eerie and dreadful darkness of visiting the site of Belsen Concentration Camp. Nor would this be strange to the young person in one of my current congregations who recently travelled past the sites of unspeakable massacres in Izyum Forest in the Ukraine.

Such darkness is not always the near-tangible darkness of the demonic. It is also with the man who had an industrial accident twenty years ago, his health barely recovered and every failed relationship now drawn into the narrative of his own internal rage. It is the family who see no way to escape the weight of debt and so, to numb the pain, spend even more. It is the boy whose dad died young and who now fights against every teacher, every older sibling, every grandparent who tries to help. And, terrifyingly, the darkness is still closer to home: the line between good and evil passes, as Soviet dissident Aleksandr Solzhenitsyn once observed, through every human heart. This too is darkness which must be confronted and not ignored.

In attending to darkness, we also must address the role of mainline churches in the theft of land from indigenous peoples. It is difficult to overstate the disastrous effect of this on indigenous peoples, and on the mission of the Church. When the message of the gospel reached the Māori of Aotearoa (New Zealand) in the nineteenth century, its message flourished and, in contrast to many Pākehā (Europeans), the newcomers to the faith 'practised what they preached'. But, as Jay Ruka has written, 'Such glory days were to pass because of one particular issue: land.'[10] Sometimes the Church and its missionaries attempted to defend the rights of indigenous peoples, but on too many occasions they colluded with theft and the desecration of place. In the case of my own denomination, the Church's sanction of land theft sometimes happened directly, as during the Highland and Lowland clearances of the nineteenth century, or also indirectly, when its members supported the colonisation of other lands. Not to remember this dark history is a perpetuation of injustice and also, in the words of Jay Ruka, an act of 'amnesia' which prevents us moving to a fairer future.[11]

The darkness, as Jesus and the prophets showed, cannot be left alone. In the Old Testament we are told the troubled story of the city of Jericho. After this city has been destroyed by the Israelites their leader, Joshua, places a curse on anyone who might attempt to rebuild it, in particular that their eldest and youngest children will die (Josh. 6:26). Hundreds of years later, a builder called Hiel attempts this very thing, but Joshua's curse still holds, and his eldest and youngest children do indeed die. Though the city is rebuilt, over the following years something bad still resides in this accursed place: the water is bad, the land unfruitful, and mothers miscarry. Yet more years later, the prophet Elisha hears of these calamities, and at last an individual with sufficient spiritual power resolves to do something. He finds the source of the city's water and throws salt on it. Immediately the water is healed, and Elisha pronounces that from now on 'neither death nor miscarriage shall come from it' (Josh. 6:26; 1 Kings 16:34; 2 Kings 2:19–22). The curse of place is, at last, undone.

Oh that bringing of healing to our contemporary cities was as easy as throwing salt into the water supply. But still we must seek such transformation. In the late 1960s, Richard Holloway and John Harvey were part of the Gorbals group, a faith community committed to living in solidarity with the people in one of Glasgow's poorest parishes. Richard, at that time the local episcopal priest, was struggling with colossal doubt and could think of nothing honest to say about Jesus' resurrection in his forthcoming Easter service. At ten to midnight on Holy Saturday he phoned his neighbour John, who crossed the street to try and figure out what the resurrection meant on that particular Easter in the Gorbals. Aided by a small amount of whisky, they came up with the following answer: resurrection is a transformation to be lived.[12] This is the nature of parish work in relation to darkness: to see every place and every moment as an occasion for resurrection, a transformation which is to be lived. This may mean community meals and warm spaces, it may mean anti-poverty projects and youth empowerment projects, it may mean the simplest of things: a visit, a conversation, a prayer. Anything which lives with a certain holy defiance – that the darkness will not be dark for ever; that this is a place where the resurrection can become real. Just recently, the Church of Scotland moderator visited our local anti-debt project, and at the end of the visit she fell into conversation with one of the project's clients. Given our timetable, I imagined this would only be a two-minute conversation. Forty-five minutes later, they were both still talking. That conversation, many minutes longer than scheduled, turned out to be a turning point in that individual's life: she now has a new confidence and a sense of future. This was an utterly ordinary thing: a conversation, albeit with an individual who in that moment was possessed of unusual spiritual insight and power. But we in the main-line hold that our moderators are no different from any other believer; they are first among equals. In the face of darkness, all of us are called to be an agent of resurrection, that continually recurring transformation which is to be lived.

Connectedness

Around the 1960s the Church began to erase a word which had proved excessively harmful to the wellbeing of our planet: 'dominion'. Dominion, according to various translations of Genesis 1, was to characterise humanity's relationship with creation, a relationship in which we would dominate and subdue (Gen. 1:28–31). In the late Middle Ages, this Christian concept of dominion set in motion the unrestrained ploughing, quarrying, deforesting and hunting which birthed the catastrophic ecological crisis of today.[13] A heart-breaking example of dominion's catastrophic effects was experienced by the naturalist Gavin Maxwell, who once brought two otter cubs from Nigeria to breed in Scotland. One day he was horrified to discover that one of these otters had been killed, and the other fatally wounded, by a shotgun-wielding Church of Scotland minister, whose justification for this unspeakable act was that 'the Lord gave man control over the beasts of the field'.[14]

With the havoc wrecked by dominion becoming increasingly clear, 'stewardship' became the Church's new paradigm for its relationship with the rest of creation. Stewardship reminded us that the earth was passed to humanity in sacred trust. Though a definite improvement on dominion, stewardship was a somewhat lifeless and functional word: it was the language of the fragile heirloom handed down, of the one who stores an item in a safe place, but never enjoys it. And what of the outrageous assumption that we humans might even be capable of stewarding the vastness of the oceans, the forces of the atmosphere or the complex ecosystems of the land?

Given the inadequacies of dominion and stewardship, a better word for ecological relationship has come to the fore: 'community'. This concept is not new to countless indigenous peoples, nor to anyone who has read the psalms.[15] When Jesus asks us to consider the lilies of the field (Matt. 6:28–30), he is not simply using these as an illustration; he is teaching us (in the words of the poet Wendell Berry) that 'we and the lilies are in, certain critical ways, alike'.[16] Each of us is dependent on the kindness of the Creator, and also able to respond to the gift. It is this kinship which Mary Oliver celebrates in her much-loved poem 'Wild Geese': that as the geese fly over our heads, they call to us, announcing our place 'in the family of things'.[17]

This sense of community, of creational connectedness, is open to us all. One of my favourite daily moments happens at dawn, walking round the small park opposite our house with our two spaniel dogs, just as the light is breaking over the hills but the sun cannot yet be seen. The park is surrounded by trees, and from them comes a chorus of birdsong. I used to feel like an intruder among this orchestra of thrushes, finches and blackbirds; but, more recently, in the spirit of community, I have sensed its welcome, an invitation to this riotous daily celebration, a party for the soon-to-appear sun, to hear the same call as came from Mary Oliver's wild geese – that we are all a part of the 'family of things'.

This sense of creation community ran strong within the Celtic Church, not through stating 'we are in community with creation', but in speaking as if there were no other way to understand ourselves; that we humans are co-participants with all creation in the adventure of existence and, above all, in the praise of God. Or, as the Celts expressed it:

> There is no plant in the ground
> But is full of his virtue,
> There is no form in the strand
> But it is full of His blessing …
>
> There is no bird on the wing,
> There is no star in the sky
> There is nothing beneath the sun,
> But proclaims his goodness.[18]

To live in place is to be alive to the connectedness of all creation.

The Great Magnificent 'All'

A commitment to being in parish, to 'spiritual localism'[19], involves many dynamics and practices, including those we have explored: attentiveness, lostness, darkness, hereness and connection. Its practitioners tell stories which share themes, but usually refuse generalisation. However, if there is something in common it is that parish is a place of divine encounter. To be in parish, to engage with its space, like so many of the other charisms, is sacramental.[20] To be in parish is to encounter at some point, whether as surprising interruption or long-awaited epiphany, the very presence of God.

My friends Derek and Helen have lived for many years on a housing estate in the Scottish town of Motherwell. Derek is the parish minister, and Helen works to facilitate numerous local projects; their home is always a place of hospitality and welcome. Derek and Helen sit within a long tradition of mainline ministry – that which is radically committed to being part of community over a long period of time and finds its ultimate inspiration in the story of God who, in Eugene Peterson's famous translation, 'moved into the neighbourhood' (John 1:14, MSG).

Derek tells the story of one day seeing a new minibus parked in his parish. It belonged to a large church which had recently begun outreach work in the area. Emblazoned on its side was the slogan 'Bringing God to North Motherwell'. This came as something of a shock to Derek, who believed that God might have been present in North Motherwell for quite some time, and certainly prior to the arrival of this particular minibus. To commit to parish is to celebrate the sacrament of place, to bear witness to the God who is always and already here.

In proclaiming God's presence in the 'here', we are simultaneously proclaiming God's presence in the 'everywhere'. This is the God who, being present in one person and one place, bore witness to God's presence in all things and all time (Eph. 1:10; 4:6; Col. 1:17). There is such boldness to that frequently used New Testament expression 'all things': every place is a holy place; every place will ultimately be reconciled. Somehow, by committing to the small of parish, we bear witness to all of the gospel.

That story of Richard Holloway and John Harvey in the Gorbals, pondering the meaning of the resurrection, would later inspire the Deacon Blue song and album *City of Love*, which spoke to me so powerfully during the Covid pandemic. For its writer, Ricky Ross, the song is one of hope, the hope which Richard Holloway and John Harvey reached that night before Easter, that the community might be transformed.[21] This too is the hope we embody when we commit to place: that every city, island, glen, village, estate and neighbourhood might fully become a parish of love.

15

Song

I was twelve years old when I first sang in four-part harmony. The song was a South African freedom song which had travelled from Soweto via Sweden to Scotland and, on this particular occasion, to a youth event in Dundee.[1] Never before had I sung hymns which were so bold in their combination of politics and theology (first verse – 'Freedom is coming', second verse – 'Jesus is coming'); hymns which were so quietly but determinedly committed (Thuma Mina – 'Send me, Lord') or so haunting in their lament (Senzenina – 'What have we done?'). Despite having such sparse lyrics, the emotional and intellectual range of these songs was remarkable and by the end of that youth event I knew three things: the joy of singing in harmony; faith and justice belong together; apartheid was surely doomed.

Renewal Requires Song

During the horrific years of apartheid, the black churches of South Africa had undergone a theological renewal. They had learned to refute any reading of the Bible which claimed divine support for ethnic separation. Drawing on insights from their own story, the German churches which had resisted Hitler and the liberationist churches of South America, they had reshaped their theology to affirm God's priority for justice and the worth of all people. This theological and spiritual renewal led to a profusion of song. It was said that after a long political talk, people might not understand, but after the freedom songs had been sung, people would say 'now I understand where you are coming from ... death to apartheid!'[2]

Songs rarely, by themselves, spark revival. But after the renewal has begun, after the Spirit has begun to blow, then very quickly the songs begin to emerge. It is a pattern we see in the scriptures: whether it is Miriam's 'Song of the Sea', sung after the Israelites have tasted freedom; or Mary's 'Magnificat' after the Spirit has come upon her; or the early Church's 'At the name of Jesus' (Phil. 2:6–11), renewal always leads to song.

This essential connection was not lost on Martin Luther. In the early days of the Reformation, he produced a collection of 'German Psalms' that 'the Word of God may be kept alive among the people by singing'.[3] Translated into metrical verse and set to well-known tunes, it was critical to Luther that these might be easily memorised, and thus quickly belong to all the people. Shortly afterwards, in Scotland, three Dundonian brothers by the name of Wedderburn were inspired by Luther's example to set 'Godlie rymes' to the well-known tunes of 'bawdie songs'. The subsequent 'Wedderburn' or 'Dundee' psalms became so popular that surviving copies are now exceedingly rare, not because few were printed, but because the 'Buik of Godlie Psalms and Spiritual Sangis' was nearly always worn out through extensive use. Other than the Bible, according to one eminent historian of Scottish Psalmody, this book 'did more than any other to further the Reformation cause'.[4]

The link between renewal and song is also no secret to Methodists. Their movement, born from John Wesley's 'warming of the heart', was amplified through the thousands of hymns penned by his brother Charles. Consequently, hymn-singing has always been one of the great charisms of Methodism. Just over a century after Charles Wesley's death, another Methodist hymn-writer, Enoch Sontonga, composed 'Nkosi Sikelel' iAfrika'; this is a hymn which yearns for an entire continent to be drenched in the presence of God. In the words of one commentator, this hymn 'has come to symbolise, more than any other piece of expressive culture, the struggle for African unity and liberation in South Africa'.[5]

The spiritual renewal which requires song need not be as momentous as the Reformation, or the South African liberation struggle. In 1979, John Bell, a city-wide youth worker, found himself accompanying a group of young people to a camp on the island of Iona, a place rich with the history of spiritual renewal. For these individuals, alongside dozens of their peers, this was a time of unique challenge and radical exploration of their faith. Sadly, such radicalism was not matched by the camp's worship, in which the leader's solitary gesture towards innovation was the introduction of sudden and unnatural rallentandos into the last verse of every hymn.

After only one night of this, and in despair, John prayed to God that something might be done. The next morning, he awoke to the news that this worship leader had succumbed to a mysterious illness and had, at short notice, been required to leave the island (it is assumed he subsequently made a swift recovery). Without any viable alternatives, the organisers of the camp asked if John, who at this point had lost any interest in church music, might be involved in the worship for the remainder of the week. Through changing the language of texts and using different styles of singing, the camp's young people were enabled to engage more deeply both in worship and commitment.

For John, this was the genesis of a vocation which has led to him writing, often with others, hundreds of original hymns and gathering numerous collections of songs from the world Church. Since that 1970s youth camp, he has remained convinced that new songs should be born out of specific contexts or experiences and written for a particular occasion rather than in hope of publication. Once again, contexts of transformation generate an irrepressible desire to sing a new song.

Shaping the Future

New songs not only reflect renewal but are also an essential instrument of its continuation. When, for example, the Scottish Reformation was fragile and its outcome in doubt, the new arrangements of the psalms played a critical role. In 1582, for example, when a Reformer by the name of John Durie returned to Edinburgh after a period of exile, he was met by a crowd of thousands who accompanied him to the city's St Giles' Cathedral, singing four-part psalms with such 'great sound and majestie that it moved both themselves and the huge multitude of beholders', including both Durie's supporters and his opponents. A later chronicler observed that following this great swelling of song, the repressive Duke of Lennox was 'more affrayed of this sight than anie thing that ever he had seene before in Scotland'.[6] Similarly, when the South African Church sang of freedom, the singing itself played an essential role in achieving that freedom; not for nothing has the anti-apartheid movement been dubbed 'a revolution in four-part harmony'.[7] Not only does song reflect renewal, it also sustains it.

During the years I attended the Belfast church of minister and peacemaker Ken Newell, I once complained to him about a certain worship song which we often sang and which, in my view, greedily attempted to claim that every single prophetic epoch (the days of Elijah, the days of Ezekiel, and the year of Jubilee) was being simultaneously fulfilled in 1990s Belfast. Looking me in the eye, not without sympathy but recalling two decades of struggle for Christian unity and community reconciliation, Ken said, 'Neil, for twenty years I have lost every single vote at our General Assembly and it has been so hard, but just for once, when I sing that song, it feels like the ball is going in the back of the net.' For Ken, there was something in the promise of that prophetic song that gave him courage and strength to keep moving. After the early fire of renewal has begun to dim, we require musical sustenance for the hard moments ahead.

Song and Mainline Renewal

All renewal requires song because the combination of music and language takes us beyond the bounds of logic and encompasses the heart and the imagination. Song is also democratic; it invites participation from all – not only the speaker at the front of the room. This applies to all renewal, but what of the specifics of our own mainline renewal: the need for divine encounter, the authentic growth of the self, and a diverse community discovering its even deeper unity?

Here we might learn from the global phenomenon now known as Contemporary Christian Worship, sometimes abbreviated to 'CCW'. Though its origins lie outside the mainline, the songs of Graham Kendrick, Keith and Krysten Getty, Stuart Townend, John Wimber and Darlene Zschech, to name but a few of its writers, are well known in mainline churches. Historians of CCW have compared its story to a great river with two separate sources, both of which speak to the essential dynamics of mainline renewal.[8] The first source has a definite starting point: Abbotsford in Canada. It was here, in January 1946, that a struggling Pentecostal preacher named Reg Layzell received a revelation, based on Psalm 22:3, that God was not only the object of our worship, but also present within our praise. From this moment, Layzell's preaching and leading were renewed; his emphasis on God's presence within our worship became key to the 'Latter Rain' revival a few years later and, over the following decades, the flourishing of an entire praise and worship movement.

CCW's second source, with a more diffuse beginning, arose from a growing imperative that in a rapidly changing culture Christian worship needed to adapt in order to communicate itself. This meant adopting contemporary musical forms (particularly those of western pop and its many sub-genres). In the 1990s this cultural relevance also began to take greater account of the turn to the self, with many songs celebrating the worshipper's own personal relationship with Christ: Darlene Zschech's 'Shout to the Lord', with the opening line 'My Jesus, My Saviour', being one of the best-known examples.

This subjective turn in Christian worship has not been without its critics and may sometimes be derided as 'cosmic boyfriend music'. I too used to share in such cynicism, and to prove the point I took the best-known contemporary worship book of the 1990s and calculated the proportion of songs which began with the word 'I'; this turned out to be approximately 10 per cent of the book's content. Seeking to show that the scriptures were considerably more corporate, I then counted the percentage of psalms which began with the same word: 'I'. To my great surprise, the proportion turned out to be almost exactly the same, about 10 per cent. Songs concerning the individual self are less removed from the scriptures than we occasionally sceptical mainliners might suppose. Such personal and intimate songs have often been sung in the life of the Church. Many African American spirituals, for example, are rich in individual intimacy; although this is never exclusive, with their best exponents keen to declare: 'I can mean we and us can mean me.'

With an emphasis on divine encounter and the authentic self, CCW speaks to two of the essential elements of mainline renewal. But what of that third component: the celebration of diversity within our unity? Here we will also need worship from other traditions, to give expression to the fullness of our diversity. This will require songs which reflect a diversity of genre (not only from contemporary pop), emotion (including the darker emotions which are often represented in the psalms but less frequently in contemporary worship) and theological perspective. Contemporary worship will continue to play an essential part in this (as we have said, it fulfils several essential elements in our renewal), but we also require additional voices and genres. Only in this will we fully express our essential diversity.

An individual who has already travelled this journey is the New Zealand pastor and composer Malcolm Gordon. In the mid-2010s Gordon's songs were being sung in churches all over his native New Zealand and beyond. Though still within the genre of CCW, and with a distinctly New Zealand inflection (a little of Crowded House was in there perhaps), Gordon's songs also stretched convention. 'Lead us from the certain, into your mystery' was one of his lyrics. His setting of the ancient Celtic prayer 'St Patrick's Breastplate' had brought Malcolm into several heated debates with its assertion that 'everything is sacred'. It did not claim that 'everything is nice', says Gordon, but rather that every experience remains open to the possibility of divine transformation.

However, in 2016, Malcolm Gordon had a problem: although his songs had always been written in a spirit of authenticity and had often travelled beyond the norms of their genre, he had moved still further. Of his published songs, there were only three he still liked. Malcolm had changed. He did indeed have new songs, songs which now lay closer to his soul; but he feared recording them, not least because to do so felt 'self-indulgent', and also perhaps because those who had enjoyed his earlier material would struggle to keep company with him. However, encouraged by a successful crowdfunding campaign, he decided to record. The result was the beautiful album *Thistledown*, a collection which brought faith into new territory. These are songs which live with a truthful delicacy and celebrate Christ who walks ahead of us and so often beckons us into the unknown, the unknown where he himself has always been.

We will require more of this song-writing tradition in the mainline, songs which stretch our insights, which move us into the unfamiliar (a place where we often encounter God) and more fully reflect diversity. In this spirit, two forthcoming song collections, from the Church of Scotland and the United Church of Canada, give special priority to indigenous traditions and to music from less-commercial genres.

This brings us to an essential component in the singing of new songs: it is a corporate act, involving those who write and those who sing, but also those who collect. Here we are reminded of the mainline genius for producing much-loved collections of new songs. With the advent of data projectors and photocopiers, it may have been presumed that this was an outdated gift. However, this remains as essential as ever: individual congregations and worship leaders are not able to review and assess the thousands of new songs produced each year and we need an awareness of good material which, for whatever reason, is less visible to the algorithm of a search engine.

To worship with diversity we must do the work of intentional curation. And if anyone were to object that the procedural and democratic decision-making of mainline denominations is the antithesis of such creative endeavour, then lessons should be learned from the compilation of one of the most influential collections of Christian songs ever produced: the Scottish Psalter of 1650.

As the Reformation flourished throughout Northern Europe, there had been, as we have already seen, an accompanying flurry of musical composition. During this period, composers and publishers produced numerous new editions of psalms and hymns. In addition to these public collections, countless enthusiastic amateurs would share their settings among friends. Even the King, James VI of Scotland and James I of England, attempted to force himself into this collective endeavour, although his poetic contributions were usually resisted on the grounds that they required, in the words of one contemporary critic, a 'dictionarie' to be understood.[9]

Seeking some form of uniformity across their constituent realms, a joint assembly of representatives from the Church of Scotland and the Church of England had produced, in 1646, a collection of metrical psalms which they hoped would gain general acceptance.[10] However, their efforts were rejected by the Scottish as being too English, and by the English as being too Scots.[11] Thus, in 1647, the General Assembly of the Church of Scotland decided to produce its own dedicated collection. There followed a three-year process of presbytery review, congregational review, Assembly discussion, followed by yet further revision – the exasperating like of which would be familiar to any mainline committee member. Such processes are often derided for producing bland and ineffective compromises. Not, however, in this case. Compromises were indeed struck, but these led to works of corporate genius, such as a new 23rd Psalm, which blended together the work of no fewer than seven different authors (King James did eventually get a degree of recognition – 'shall surely follow me' came from him). This was mainline committee-based decision-making at its very best. Though 'The Great Psalter' received a lukewarm early reception, over the following centuries it became definitive. Many of its settings, including that multi-author version of Psalm 23, are still frequently sung today. Our future renewal will require similarly collaborative processes if we are all to fulfil the Biblical command to 'sing a new song'.

More than Song

This chapter has focused on contemporary song, but there is ample evidence that mainline renewal will enlist a far wider range of artistic endeavour. Indeed, it is of the very essence of creativity that it radiates out in numerous and surprising directions. It will not, for example, be confined to the music of the present, but also include older music being discovered anew. St Martin-in-the-Fields Church in central London, for example, has seen an unprecedented response (from churchgoers and non-churchgoers alike) to their weekly 'Great Sacred Music' events. The visual arts will also be key. My current congregations host not one, but two, groups of quilters (with their arrays of highly impressive sewing machines), whose work ranges from landscape to abstract, and often weaves in their own personal story. Alongside those made for their own use, they have produced quilts for care-leavers and refugees. And though an eclectic mix of churchgoers and agnostics, they also frequently make connections with faith.

In my former church, Carol Marples,[12] a liturgical artist, once worked with congregation and community members to produce a stunning mural which connected faith, our area's industrial past, and our congregation's ongoing life: Christian imagery and scriptural verse were set alongside mountings of coal, plate steel and a menu board; the design even managed to incorporate a stylistically mounted vacuum cleaner, in recognition of the factory in which hundreds of local people had worked.

Peter and Heidi Gardner (Peter is Pioneer Minister for the visual arts community in Glasgow) have enabled installations in numerous congregations and also regularly at the Church of Scotland's General Assembly. In 2023, they were aware that following the challenges of Covid, the uncertainties of planning, and the larger existential questions facing all mainline denominations, the mood of the Assembly and of the whole Church was low. Instead of the large installations of previous years, they opted for something provocatively tiny, a small white badge, barely an inch in diameter. Perhaps remembering a parable of Jesus about the power of small objects, they produced an artwork to counter the prevailing despondency in which we, the people of the Church, would ourselves become the installation. On each badge they printed, in capital letters, the famous words of Julian of Norwich: 'ALL SHALL BE WELL'. Assembly commissioners were presented with a badge and invited to wear it during the debates. So it was, during challenging discussions about our potential demise, that we would also see, pinned to lapels and lanyards throughout the hall, hundreds of white badges pointing to a different possibility: 'ALL SHALL BE WELL, ALL SHALL BE WELL, ALL SHALL BE WELL, ALL SHALL BE WELL, ALL SHALL BE WELL ...'

Into God

Great art has the power to move us to the 'transcendent', to move us beyond ourselves and towards a sense of God. Regardless of the Church's frequent suspicion of the visual arts, Christians from almost every tradition have always been drawn towards light as a symbol of divine presence.[13] As an expression of this, on Midsummer's Day 2023, Peter and Heidi invited members of the public to sit in St Ninian's Episcopal Church in Glasgow. Across the building's columns they had stretched forty-six filaments of translucent line. As, outside, the sun moved across the sky and shone through the various windows, different filaments would brighten at different points of the day; each one revealed the light which was always present but which we do not always see. When the sun reached its highest point (which in Glasgow on Midsummer's Day is apparently at 1:18pm), one centrally placed filament was placed to shine with particular brightness. 'Encountering something expected, through the catalyst of contemporary art amid sacred architecture, people seemed really surprised,' says Peter; 'many stayed for hours.'

Repeatedly we forget the power of art, in its wild diversity of forms, to evoke the presence of God. As John Bell has noted, when people are asked to identify their most significant experience of worship, only one in a hundred will mention a sermon (and those who do are usually preachers). 'More commonly', he adds, 'they will talk about a song, a silence, a symbolic action, a service of worship in an unusual place.'[14] If, as we have said, the greatest calling of the Church is to be a place for divine encounter and to re-enchant a disenchanted age, then we must remember the power of the arts.

In the New Testament, it is its songs – its new songs in Philippians, Colossians, Revelation, Luke and John – which often reveal its deepest insights into the nature of God. It is in them that we hear songs of the Word who was God, the Word made flesh, the God who breaks upon us like the light of the dawn, who reconciles all things, who is worthy of all blessing and honour and glory and might. Song, like all art, does not need to equivocate or to clarify; its poetry takes risks which prose resists. This is why the New Testament's songs seem most able to reveal the mystery of God. May all the songs of the Church's tomorrow sustain our renewal and enable us to perceive the same.

16

Stillness

In seeking out the gifts of the mainline, two qualifications have been essential: that the gift has played a key part in the mainline story, and that the gift is for the good of the Church and of the world. Our final gift of stillness is clearly the second, and much less obviously the first.

In our hurried world, we are hungry for stillness. We need an antidote to the pressures of work and expectation, to the avarice appetite which technology (and particularly social media) has for our time, and patterns of family life in which parents and carers are expected to spend much longer periods of time with their children.[1]

However, stillness does not seem to appear much in the mainline tradition, for we are children of the much-vaunted Protestant work ethic. Most contemporary writing on stillness comes from Catholic sources. Perhaps we Protestants will simply have to borrow a gift we have never previously owned – until we remember that there actually *is* a charism of stillness, which has indeed played a huge role in the Protestant story. But we in the mainline have forgotten it or, rather, recall it with such unhappy memories that we have little desire to reclaim this particular item of lost property. The name of this unloved gift of stillness? Sabbath.

What went wrong with Sabbath? Many of us will have our own particular testimonies of Sabbath misery: it may have been a tied-up pair of football boots, deemed off-limits for the day; padlocked swings in the local municipal park or board games locked away for twenty-four hours. For me, the defining memory of Sabbath is of a particular pair of boyhood trousers, the only pair which were smart enough to be worn in church, but which were made of a particularly rough brown fabric, which meant that wearing them felt like my legs were wrapped in nettles for eighteen hours. I absolutely hated these trousers, and even writing of them now I can feel my body tense.

My mother was clearly not oblivious to my protests and did her best to retrieve the situation, sewing into these trousers a lining which took the prickliness away, but this also rendered them freezing cold for the first five minutes that I wore them. Despite this improvement, those trousers remained for many years a continued symbol of my dislike of Sunday, and also – if truth be told – a wariness of whichever god had wished me to be wearing such painfully uncomfortable clothing on his behalf.

With such unhappy memories of the Sabbath, it is little wonder that in recent years mainline Protestants have moved from Sabbatarian discipline to Sabbatarian indifference. One recent American survey found that, in comparison to their evangelical or Catholic siblings, 'liberal' and 'moderate' Protestants were far less likely to observe Sabbath.[2] Somewhere in the mainline Protestant journey, Sabbath moved from being a hairshirt to a garment we rarely wear. First, we forgot that 'the sabbath was made for humankind, and not humankind for the sabbath' (Mark 2:27), and then we simply forgot Sabbath altogether.

However, with our perpetually busy and inattentive lives, in a culture which has forgotten the value of slow, we mainliners urgently need to recover this gift which the poet Chaim Machman Bialik once called 'the most brilliant creation of the Hebrew spirit'.[3] For the value of Sabbath has not been forgotten by those to whom it was first given. Late Friday afternoon in modern-day Jerusalem is a time when an already busy city becomes even busier. Cars drive past faster than ever, pedestrians pick up their pace, buses start moving before new passengers have had a chance to sit down; the city is in a flurry, and why? Everybody needs to be indoors by the time that Sabbath begins. 'Jerusalem on Friday,' says writer A. J. Swoboda, 'is a whole city coming home.'[4] The effect of this wholehearted commitment to Sabbath, to a weekly day of celebration and rest, is remarkable. To quote one Gentile journalist who had recently moved to Israel, 'Now that I'm used to it, I'm all for it and think if they'd shut down the whole world for the week, we wouldn't be in the mess we're in.'[5]

Another group with a similar degree of Sabbath commitment are the Seventh Day Adventists. Their wholehearted observance is a principal reason why they live, on average, for ten years longer than their peers.[6] Both Jews and Seventh Day Adventists have remembered that Sabbath is neither a restriction nor a constriction, but instead the most valuable gift.

When observant Jews sit down on a Friday night to begin Sabbath, they often light two candles, one for each of the Jewish law's two Sabbath commandments. The first candle is for the Exodus commandment: that Sabbath be kept in imitation of God's resting on the seventh day. This is the candle of rest. The second candle is for the Deuteronomy commandment: that the Sabbath be kept in memory of the people's deliverance from slavery. This is the candle of freedom.[7] Each of these deserves further attention.

The Candle of Rest

In the Genesis account of creation, we read that on the seventh day God finished creation (Gen. 2:2–3). The idea that God finished creation on the seventh day is suggestive of more than one interpretation. The first is that God purposefully completed anything which had been left unfinished from the previous six days. This idea seems to be present in some of Jesus' highly frequent Sabbath healings – especially the healing of the blind man in John 9. This is Sabbath that pays attention to endings and completings, for we do not live continuously but episodically. We need a rhythm which is about starting and finishing, rather than always doing. There is something about Sabbath which places a proper full-stop on to the previous six days.

The other interpretation of 'finished' is that rest itself has a completing quality: that the choice not to be active enables a hidden, silent power to bring our labours to completion, a completion which would never have been possible had we chosen to stay busy. Thus, Sabbath renders us more fruitful, not less. It is an act of handing over our labours to the hidden work of God. It is thus a symbol both of our own limits, and of our trust in the God who is not far off, but who continuously holds our life.

We are called to exercise this trust without exception. This means we rest when we can afford the time, but also when we are under the greatest pressure. We commit to Sabbath, precisely when we experience the greatest temptation to break it. For, paradoxically, it is when we are busiest that we can least afford not to stop. And when we rest, not only is the work completed, but somehow, also, are we.

We need Sabbath, and in this hurried age we need it as never before. But in practical terms, what does a commitment to Sabbath entail? In the words of A. J. Swoboda, it is an 'opposite day'.[8] If ordinarily we drive, then it is a day for walking; if our work involves sitting, then Sabbath is a day for sport or physical activity; if our work involves care for others, then Sabbath is a day when, if possible, we are the ones to be cared for. Depending on our particular circumstances, observance on a Saturday or Sunday may not be possible, but it should remain a weekly event. And regardless of the particularities, Sabbath should always be an act of wholehearted commitment; it should always make us appear a little bit fanatical. In A. J. Swoboda's household, for example, only one phone is switched on throughout the day, and this only for reasons of emergency contact. Most friends and family are supportive, but to some this is the strangest of behaviour.

Daily Stillness

The power of weekly stillness brings us to the power of daily stillness; for the command to be still and know that God is God (Ps. 46:10) is a command for every day, not only for Sabbath. Daily stillness is a practice in which contemporary Protestants (with some notable exceptions, such as the Quakers) have much to learn from Catholic, Orthodox and, in particular, from monastic traditions. It is these which teach us, in the words of the spiritual writer Henri Nouwen, to 'fashion our own desert where we can withdraw every day, shake off our compulsions, and dwell in the gentle healing presence of our Lord'.[9]

Such practices may include scriptural contemplation (such as *Lectio Divina*, which we met in Chapter 12), the repetition of what is called the 'Jesus Prayer' ('Lord Jesus Christ, Son of God, have mercy on me a sinner'),[10] or 'Centering prayer' which is a method of giving prolonged attention to the presence of God.[11] One recent study on 'Prayer and Subjective Well-being' found that, alongside prayers of thanksgiving and adoration, prayers of contemplation were the forms of prayer which had the greatest positive effect on those who prayed them.[12] Contemplation and stillness do not, it should be stressed, involve falling into some form of trance. They often feel very ordinary, and yet through them, almost undetected, God will be at work.

In the course of researching this book, it struck me how frequently individuals, to whom I would be speaking about another of the mainline gifts, would, without prompting, refer to the essential importance of contemplative prayer and meditation in their lives. In these moments I would be reminded again of the generative nature of stillness. The people who do the most depend on regular moments of doing nothing.

What We Fear

We should also note one of the more difficult aspects of contemplative prayer, and of stillness in general. When we are properly still, the darker rumblings of the soul begin to rise to the surface. Our perpetual busy-ness has kept these suppressed for years, but now at last they have a chance to make themselves known. We subconsciously know this, for the avoidance of these more difficult thoughts and emotions is one of our primary motivations to keep busy. The moment when our darkest thoughts arise is a moment when, in the words of that great poet of Sabbath, Wendell Berry, 'What I am afraid of comes. I live for a while in its sight.' The temptation here is to give up, partly because we are ashamed of our thoughts, and the stillness seems not to be working, but we must have the courage to stay. As Berry writes, when 'I live for a while in its sight. What I fear in it leaves me, and the fear of it leaves me.'[13] The advice from all the great teachers is also, especially at this point, to find someone appropriate to talk to. Stillness should be practised, where possible, alongside at least one other person who has walked the path before.[14]

This is the first Sabbath candle, the candle of rest. The candle of the hidden work of stillness, in which creation is brought to mysterious completion.

The Candle of Freedom

The second Sabbath candle takes its meaning from the book of Deuteronomy 5:15: 'Remember that you were a slave in the land of Egypt, and the Lord your God brought you out from there with a mighty hand and an outstretched arm; therefore the Lord your God commanded you to keep the sabbath day.'

In his sustained reflection on the Sabbath, 'Sabbath as Resistance', Old Testament scholar Walter Brueggemann sees today's market-driven economy as a modern-day Egypt.[15] For him, the keeping of Sabbath is an ongoing act of resistance to the enslaving forces of the economy: it is resistance to anxiety, coercion, exclusivism (for everyone in Israel is welcomed into Sabbath), multitasking and covetousness. Thus, Sabbath becomes a daring reclamation of our God-given identity, in resistance to a culture which reduces human life to the requirements of the market.

Brueggemann's linkage of market-driven economics with the Jewish memory of Egyptian slavery is a powerful and prophetic word. But there may be, alas, another institution whose exhausting routines, relentless demand for more and spirit-sapping practices might also echo the insatiable demands of Pharaoh. For too often, the Church has not behaved as liberator, but as slave-master; and its rhythms have not been pro-Sabbath, but anti-Sabbath. Furthermore, during a period of institutional decline,[16] the anti-Sabbath tendencies of the Church's life can become even more pronounced. Here, our unit of production is not the Egyptian brick but the programme, the service, the meeting, the new recruit. And with fewer resources, we are now attempting to meet our previous quotas of demand, but to make these 'without straw' (Exod. 5:1–21). When the targets are not met, the taskmasters demand to know 'why?' and the pharaohs of our subconscious mind scream 'lazy, lazy, lazy'.

When training to be a minister, I will never forget the seminar on self-care in which our speaker, a usually placid individual, suddenly erupted into fury as he told us, 'You are not Jesus!', adding, 'His ministry only lasted into his thirties, and even he had to rest. Your ministries will last much longer, how much more must you take time off.' Several years later, I discovered what may have lain at the root of his uncharacteristic ferocity. One of his greatest friends had been a renowned religious and civic leader, someone who had insisted on a life of constant availability. Despite numerous warnings to take time off, this remarkable man had died at too young an age. I later wondered if the terrible memory of his friend's death had motivated our speaker's unusual forcefulness that day. Neglect of Sabbath is highly dangerous.

In this book I have often been conscious that an aspiration for 'renewal' can easily slide into a demand for 'success', and that a Church which craves success, in particular through rising numbers, will seek to turn its people into slaves, who must work until they collapse exhausted.

How do we prevent renewal becoming yet another initiative which asks us to give even more? The divinely prescribed anti-dote to slavery is Sabbath. Not a Sabbath which is instituted as a nice-to-have element in a wider programme of reform, nor a Sabbath which is kept only if we have first met the scheduled targets of the previous six days. It is striking that straight after God has given the Israelites their first ever 'programme of work', he immediately follows this with a strident reiteration of the importance of Sabbath (Exod. 31:1–17). The Sabbath is to be kept 'above all' as some translations put it (Exod. 31:13, ESV, MSG).

In any strategy, programme or vision for Church renewal, the condition which must be met 'above all things' is the retention of Sabbath. If such a programme denies Sabbath to its participants, then it is not a programme of renewal, it is a return to Egypt. It should immediately be abandoned; it is Pharaoh in disguise.

Only approaches which honour Sabbath for all their participants ('your son or your daughter, your male workers, your female workers, your ox, your donkey, the stranger within your gates' – Exod. 20:10; Deut. 5:14, my own translation) will lead us into the land of freedom, the land where we live with God. In doing so, any aspiration for renewal will also incorporate a deliberate relinquishment of control, a deliberate silencing of the voice which says, 'all this depends on you', a deliberate act of resistance to the forces of disenchantment. In keeping Sabbath, we are holding space for God, the God who is never far off, the God who inhabits all space and the God who inhabits all time. And that includes times of stillness: times when it seems that absolutely nothing is happening, times when unseen, unforced and unperceived, God is bringing about our renewal.

Finding Our Voice

I think of a ragged man, spluttering and burnt, crawling through the waves and up the sands of a beach. His head spinning with religious words, only half of which he probably believes. He slowly opens his eyes because where he has been it was dark, and he is not used to the brightness of the sun. Pushing down on the sand, he brings his legs up behind him. Standing a little straighter, he peers beyond the sand to the grass, and in the distance he sees a path: a path which he must walk.

He does not yet understand everything; he is barely ready to travel the journey which the voice has asked him to make. But he has enough to live, and that is better than three days ago when he was plunging into the deepest depths.

Jesus once seemed to suggest that this is what resurrection looks like. Resurrection is about having enough to live. It is not about knowing the future, but it is about having one. Within himself, Jonah has enough. He has heard enough, and he has seen enough, and now he will walk, and he will speak, and in his walking and his speaking worlds will change. This is what resurrection looks like.

And perhaps this is us. Wearied, darkened and unsure. But we are not dead, and for the road ahead we will have enough, not only enough to survive but enough for the strange adventure of being alive.

This has been a book about a particularly stretched and wearied part of the Church, its glories apparently passed, but tentatively hopeful of a future. This will be a future of divine encounter, of being saved, of discovering our authentic selves, of diversity in our communities, of wrestling with our structures and of reclaiming our most precious gifts. This is our path: to speak the word we have been given, to transform worlds, to be alive. This is what resurrection looks like. This is what it is to find our voice.

Acknowledgements

There are a whole group of people who played a part in this book, and to whom huge thanks are due.

Thank you to Christine Smith, Mary Matthews, Linda Carroll, Michael Addison, Joanne Hill and all at Saint Andrew Press who have coached a complete beginner, taken the manuscript, helped shape it, caught numerous mistakes and turned it into the book before you. Thank you, a lot, to Liam Fraser and Linda Cracknell for crucial early advice and ongoing encouragement.

Thanks to those who first looked at the earliest drafts and were not hesitant to inform me of the need for some fairly serious editing: to John Bell who carefully dissected and then gave me the keys for putting everything back together again; to my fellow podcasters Fiona and Jen who prevented me disappearing into a warren of my own geekery; to Neil Dougall who has always encouraged and pointed me to some key texts in the area of change; to Lynn McChlery who is sharp as a tack and generous to a fault and who, alongside Stuart, gave me a place in which to write; and to Nikki Macdonald who knows of many things which happened and why they did.

To those who have been great companions in this endeavour, not least Tim and Julie, Sarah, Doug, Andrew, Ivor and Anna, Marjory, Michael, David, David and Maggie, Peter, Tommy, Morag and Andrew, Pete and Sheona and all the Grays – alongside the brilliant support of friends in Highland Perthshire and the support of the remarkable congregations of Aberfeldy, Dull & Weem, Grandtully, Logierait and Strathtay, and Tenandry, and my former congregation of Flemington Hallside; and if I might name two individuals, it would be Judy Ewer and Gillian Cahill who have so often kept me right. Much here has been learned from those in the former Ministry Council, the D10 group and Seeds for Growth; and with the beautiful people of the Abernethy Trust, the GKExperience and the various incarnations of the Wild Goose Worship Group/Resource Group/ Collective.

A huge thank you to those who have given of their time and their stories and their wisdom – in Scotland: Adrian Armstrong, Grant Barclay, Alex Bauer, Lynsey Brennan, Suzi Farrant, Sandy Forsyth, Sally Foster Fulton, Peter Gardner, Thora and Ronnie Glencorse, John and Molly Harvey, John Hayward, Martin Johnstone, Alison Kennedy, John Kewley, Beth Kirkland, Anne Logan, Iain McLarty, Phill Mellstrom, John and Mary Miller, Bill Mitchell, Derek and Helen Pope, Andrew and Amy Rooney, Ricky Ross, John Russell, Mark Sime, Pam and Paul Skrgatic, David Stewart, Gordon Strang, Alison, Robert and Rima Swinfen, Fiona Tweedie, Foy Vance, Michael Worobec; to Peter Brierley, Sally Mann and Jo Williams in England; to those living on the blessed Island of Ireland: Rob Clements, Ken Newell, Pádraig Ó Tuama and Jan and Matt Peach; to those wonderful residents of the Americas: Tod Bolsinger, Mary Kay DuChene, Susan Jackson, Catherine Faith MacLean, Susan Nienaber, Steve Salyards, Adam Shelton, Lydia Sohn, Joanna Symonds, Mark Sundby; and to some truly inspiring inhabitants of Aotearoa: Malcolm Gordon and Mo Morgan. To any I have omitted, my sincere apologies.

To all of the above, the good bits belong to you, and the remainder lands on me.

I owe a huge debt of gratitude to my wife Anna who has been a source of constant support, patience and love through these many hours of writing and editing, and to our children, Sam, Zoe and Susie, who make me smile and just so grateful for the human beings they are; and to Graeme, Anne and Ruth who know what I'm really like.

This book is dedicated to my parents, Robert and Elizabeth Glover, who have influenced its contents more than they could possibly know, and in memory of the most brilliant human being, Graham Maule, whose spirit has animated so many of its pages.

Notes

Introduction

1 Here I am using a standard definition of 'mainline' to refer to theologically broad Protestant denominations. See James Hudnut-Beumler and Mark Silk, *The Future of Mainline Protestantism in America*, New York: Columbia University Press, 2018, 3–4.

Chapter 1: Loss

1 These are countries in which statistics are more readily available. In countries such as Australia and Switzerland, anecdotal evidence would suggest similar trends.

2 Based on the work of leadership writers Ronald Heifetz and Marty Linsky. For application to a church context, see Gil Rendle, *Quietly Courageous*, Lanham, MD: Rowman and Littlefield, 2019; and Tod Bolsinger, *Canoeing the Mountains*, Downers Grove, IL: InterVarsity Press, 2015.

3 This conclusion is based on the work of Andrew Root and Blair Bertrand in *When Church Stops Working*, Grand Rapids, MI: Brazos Press, 2023.

4 Conversely, where mainline churches exist in non-secular countries – for example, in sub-Saharan Africa, South America and South Asia – they have continued to experience growth.

5 Possible reasons why Secularisation took greater effect in Protestant countries include a history of schism leading to religiously fractured societies (see Liam J. Fraser, *Mission in Contemporary Scotland*, Edinburgh: Saint Andrew Press, 2021, 38–43) and a refusal to believe in the enchantment of the Catholic Mass, leading to an ensuing Disenchantment within many other aspects of existence. See James K. A. Smith, *How (Not) To Be Secular*, Grand Rapids, MI: Eerdmans, 2014, 39.

6 For more on these dimensions of Secularism, see Charles Taylor, *A Secular Age*, Cambridge, MA: Belknap Press, 2007, 1–3, and the helpful summary in Smith, *Secular*, 20–3.

7 Fraser, *Mission*, 44–5, notes two studies of Church of Scotland congregations in the 1950s and 1960s: attendance was overwhelm-

ingly motivated by concerns for morality and respectability, with only 13 per cent of members attending for reasons of worship. Competence and professionalism were the qualities most sought in prospective elders, significantly more than the need for a personal faith.

8 Their subsequent description and analysis of this work is published as Paul Heelas and Linda Woodhead, *The Spiritual Revolution*, Oxford: Blackwell Publishing, 2005.

9 Barbara Brown Taylor, *The Preaching Life*, Norwich: Canterbury Press, 2013, 3–5.

10 Joseph Bottum writing in 'First Things' in 2008, cited at https://www.firstthings.com/article/2008/08/the-death-of-protestant-america (accessed 21.1.24).

11 Robert W. Jenson, *A Theology in Outline: Can These Bones Live?*, New York: Oxford University Press, 2016, 30.

Chapter 2: God

1 In this context, Reformed refers to those churches, including all Presbyterian churches, which trace their roots back to the teaching of John Calvin.

2 Andrew Root and Blair Bertrand, *When Church Stops Working*, Grand Rapids, MI: Brazos Press, 2023, 7.

3 James K. A. Smith, *Desiring the Kingdom*, Grand Rapids, MI: Baker Academic, 2009, 40.

4 Quoted in John Ortberg, *God Is Closer Than You Think*, Grand Rapids, MI: Zondervan, 2005, 17–18; this section is heavily indebted to John Ortberg's writing on this subject.

5 This section is hugely indebted to Charles Taylor's chapter on 'Providential Deism', in his *A Secular Age*, Cambridge, MA: Belknap Press, 2007, 221–69, or, for a more accessible account, see James K. A. Smith, *How (Not) To Be Secular*, Grand Rapids, MI: Eerdmans, 2014, 53–7.

6 Liam J. Fraser, *Mission in Contemporary Scotland*, Edinburgh: Saint Andrew Press, 2021, 45.

Chapter 3: Seek

1 Julian of Norwich, Divine Revelations, Book X, available online at https://www.documentacatholicaomnia.eu/03d/1343-1398,_Julian._of_Norwich,_Revelations_Of_Divine_Love,_EN.pdf (accessed 21.1.24).

2 Alexander Carmichael, *Carmina Gadelica: Hymns and Incantations*, Edinburgh: Floris, 1992, 204–5.

3 Tommy MacNeil, *Sleeping Giant*, River Publishing, 2021, 42–4.

4 Annie Dillard, *Teaching a Stone to Talk*, New York: Harper Perennial, 1983, 52.

5 See Lester Ruth and Lim Swee Hong, *A History of Contemporary Christian Worship*, Grand Rapids, MI: Baker Academic, 2021, on this twin history.

6 In this section I am greatly indebted to John Philip Newell's reflection on the life of John Muir in *Sacred Earth Sacred Soul*, London: William Collins, 2021, 149–69.

7 There is some doubt as to whether Robertson completed his climb of one of the Munros (Scottish mountains over 3,000 feet) but he is still listed as the first official Munroist.

8 Alastair McIntosh, *Poacher's Pilgrimage*, Edinburgh: Birlinn, 2023, especially 31–5.

9 Charles Taylor, *A Secular Age*, Cambridge, MA: Belknap Press, 2007, 79–80 and 231.

10 Barbara Brown Taylor, *An Altar in the World*, Norwich: Canterbury Press, 2009, 30.

Chapter 4: Saved

1 The Greek words for faith, or having faith, are sometimes translated into English as 'belief' or 'believe'; however, in Greek it is the same underlying word.

2 Matt has since greatly improved ... me, not so much.

3 The details of Cram's life are drawn from David M. Guss, *The 21 Escapes of Lt Alastair Cram*, London: Macmillan, 2018.

4 Charles Taylor, *A Secular Age*, Cambridge, MA: Belknap Press, 2007, 7–8.

5 UNESCO is the United Nations Educational, Scientific and Cultural Organization, aimed at 'promoting world peace and security through international cooperation in education, arts, sciences and culture'.

Chapter 5: Me

1 Paul Heelas and Linda Woodhead, *The Spiritual Revolution*, Oxford: Blackwell Publishing, 2005, 2–3.

2 Heelas and Woodhead, *Spiritual Revolution*, 5.

3 Charles Taylor, *A Secular Age*, Cambridge, MA: Belknap Press, 2007, 513.

4 As one of my old teachers, who was a strict churchgoer, put it in our sixth-year yearbook.

5 See Doug Gay, *Reforming the Kirk*, Edinburgh: Saint Andrew Press, 2017, 15.

6 Pádraig Ó Tuama, *Poetry Unbound*, Edinburgh: Canongate Books, 2022, 21.

7 Cited in Carl R. Trueman, *The Rise and Triumph of the Modern Self*, Wheaton, IL: Crossway, 2020, 57.

8 For an extremely helpful analysis of identity and the politics of recognition (even if I do not agree with every conclusion), see Trueman, *Rise and Triumph*, 56–64.

9 James Finley, *Merton's Palace of Nowhere*, Notre Dame, IN: Ave Maria Press, 1978, 127; the original quote uses 'Himself' rather than 'themselves'.

10 Rowan Williams, *Being Disciples*, London: SPCK, 2016, 51.

11 Although the original Hebrew of this verse refers to 'you' plural, the more subjective 'you' singular is more naturally inferred from the English.

12 Heelas and Woodhead, *Spiritual Revolution*, 18–23. Though much smaller in number, Heelas and Woodhead also surveyed congregations of 'experiential humanity'; these congregations were Unitarian, Quaker or Christian Scientist.

13 There have been several trenchant critiques of this form of church life, especially in the light of several high-profile failures. I do not dispute many of these objections, but still hold that the attention to self within Evangelical-Charismatic churches has much to teach the mainline church.

Chapter 6: Conservatives

1 This is a key argument of Kristin Kobes Du Mez in *Jesus and John Wayne*, New York: Liveright, 2021.

2 For example, a 2016 census of Scottish churches showed that the number of evangelical Christians was slightly rising, whereas in the previous decade and a half the number of those describing themselves as 'liberal' or 'broad' had almost halved. The 2010 Faith Communities Today survey in North America found that belonging to a conservative denomination was the single most significant correlative of growth.

3 The results of this are reviewed in C. Kirk Hadaway, Facts on Growth 2010, available from www.faithcommunitiestoday.org (21.1.24).

4 For a comprehensive survey of UK church statistics see https://www.brierleyconsultancy.com (21.1.24).

5 See the 2022 study by the Public Religion Research Institute at https://www.prri.org/research/religion-and-congregations-in-a-time-of-social-and-political-upheaval/ (21.1.24).

6 See Liam J. Fraser, *Mission in Contemporary Scotland*, Edinburgh: Saint Andrew Press, 2021, 118–22; and also Harry Reid, *Outside Verdict*, Edinburgh: Saint Andrew Press, 2002.

7 Here I am equating the Beloved Disciple of the Fourth Gospel with the apostle John. There is not unanimous agreement on this from New Testament scholars, but the Church tradition, the closeness of John to Jesus in the other Gospels, plus John's mysterious absence from the Fourth Gospel, suggests for me they are the same individual.

8 Cited in Tom Holland, *Dominion*, London: Abacus, 2020, 243.

9 Fraser, *Mission*, 38–43.

10 Katie Cross, 'I Have the Power in My Body to Make People Sin': The Trauma of Purity Culture and the Concept of "Body Theodicy"', in Karen O'Donnell and Katie Cross, eds, *Feminist Trauma Theologies*, London: SCM Press, 2020.

11 I should also add that this is not a universal experience. I also have friends who have been nearly destroyed by the insatiable demand for more which they experienced within an evanglical-charismatic fellowship.

12 John Hayward, 'Mathematical Modeling of Church Growth', *Journal of Mathematical Sociology*, 23(4), 1999, 255–92.

13 Fraser, *Mission*, 120–1.

14 Dietrich Bonhoeffer, *The Cost of Discipleship*, London: SCM Press, 2015, Chapter 1, paras 6–7.

15 Quoted at https://sluggerotoole.com/2015/11/30/remembering-the-life-of-fr-gerry-reynolds/ (21.1.24).

Chapter 7: Middle

1 Civil partnerships were at that time the only legally recognised partnerships open to same-gender couples. They could only be formed through a secular ceremony, but some ministers had performed blessing services.

2 Robert Gagnon's writing in this area can be accessed at www.robgagnon.net (21.1.24) and in Robert Gagnon, *The Bible and Homosexual Practice*, Nashville, TN: Abingdon Press, 2002.

3 James Alison, *Faith Beyond Resentment*, London: Darton, Longman and Todd, 2001, 98.

4 Church of Scotland reports at that time had adopted the terms 'traditionalist' and 'revisionist'.

5 Almost all of these leaders subsequently left the denomination.

6 John and Mary don't recall any mention of Croatia in this conversation, and they have never been there. This seems to diminish the 'coincidence level' of this story; however, ten years later, none of the other participants can remember any other country being mentioned. I certainly 'heard' Croatia (as is borne out from texts from the time), and now am even more perplexed as to why the name of this country entered my consciousness at this point.

7 It is this story which played a crucial part in worship leader Vicky Beeching's affirming her own sexuality; see Vicky Beeching, *Undivided*, London: William Collins, 2018, 167–72. It was also a pivotal story for leading US evangelical David Gushee, and many with whom he made his own transition, described in David P. Gushee, *Changing Our Mind*, 3rd edn, Canton, MI: Read the Spirit Books, 2017, 107–8, 164.

8 This thinking underpins much of the Archbishop of Canterbury's 'Difference' course, see https://difference.rln.global/ (21.1.24).

Chapter 8: Structures

1 These are sometimes referred to as the 'Powers Trilogy' although Wink went on to write more than three such volumes. Their titles include *Naming the Powers, Unmasking the Powers, Engaging the Powers* and *The Powers that Be*. A good starter is Walter Wink, *Naming the Powers*, Philadelphia, PA: Fortress Press, 1984.

2 This section is based on the work of public health practitioner Carol Craig in *The Tears that Made the Clyde*, Glendareul: Argyll Publishing, 2010, 63–4.

3 I am particularly indebted to my colleague Neil Dougall for this section. His ideas build on the work of Gordon Smith in his book *Institutional Intelligence*, Downers Grove, IL: InterVarsity Press, 2017.

4 In particular, Craig Dykstra and James Hudnut-Beumler, cited in Graham Reside's Introduction to James Hudnut-Beumler and Mark Silk, eds, *The Future of Mainline Protestantism in America*, New York: Columbia University Press, 2018, 8.

5 Much of this section is based on the work of James Alison, *Faith Beyond Resentment*, London: Darton, Longman and Todd, 2001, 165–9.

6 Heifetz and Wheatley are quoted in Tod Bolsinger, *Canoeing the Mountains*, Downers Grove, IL: InterVarsity Press, 2015, 65–6. For Margaret Wheatley's superb article 'Leadership in the Age of Complexity: from Hero to Host', see https://www.margaretwheatley.com/articles/Leadership-in-Age-of-Complexity.pdf (21.1.24).

7 Andrew Root and Blair Bertrand, *When Church Stops Working*, Grand Rapids, MI: Brazos Press, 2023, 6.

8 Most scholars agree that Proverbs 22:17—23:11 is an adaption of earlier Egyptian 'leadership theory'.

9 There is much discussion about the difference between mission and vision, but here we employ the distinction that vision is 'what we hope to become' and mission is 'what we do to get there'.

10 Root and Bertrand, *When Church Stops Working*, 104–8.

11 It is a core component of Tod Bolsinger's *Canoeing the Mountains* and Gil Rendle's *Quietly Courageous*, Lanham, MD: Rowman and Littlefield, 2019, to give two examples.

12 Charles Wesley, 'Soldiers of Christ Arise'.

13 Much of the initial work was done in a remote bothy in Glen Kin, on Scotland's Cowal peninsula, thus 'GK'.

Chapter 9: Charisms

1 I am grateful to Tod Bolsinger for suggesting the language of charisms as an alternative to the language of DNA. Based on its usage in the Catholic tradition, Bolsinger tends to use the singular, charism. For more, see https://glenmary.org/our-story/our-founders-vision-mission/father-

bishops-charism/the-theological-concept-of-the-charism-of-a-founder/ (accessed 3.1.24).

2 There is some evidence that Billy Graham's later emphasis on social justice was strongly influenced by the critique which was made at this time by various Scottish church leaders; see Alexander Forsyth, *Mission by the People*, Eugene, OR: Pickwick, 2017, 56.

3 Although a number of trends had shown a decline since the early 1950s (specifically the numbers of new members in the Church of Scotland), it was only in 1957 that overall Church of Scotland membership entered decline, with a number of other denominations also seeing the beginning of decline in this period. I am hugely grateful for the work of John Hayward for his detailed analysis of this period.

4 Cited in Forsyth, *Mission*, 50; Forsyth's work on the history of Tom Allan and the Tell Scotland movement gives an excellent and detailed discussion of the issues outlined here.

5 Walter Brueggemann has written of this in many places, including in *Deep Memory, Exuberant Hope*, Minneapolis, MN: Fortress Press, 2000, 69–75.

Chapter 10: Connection

1 Cited in Graham Reside's 'The State of Contemporary Mainline Protestantism', in James Hudnut-Beumler and Mark Silk, eds, *The Future of Mainline Protestantism in America*, New York: Columbia University Press, 2018, 53–4. For a helpful online introduction see https://www. socialcapitalresearch.com/what-is-bridging-social-capital/ (21.1.24).

2 To paraphrase Robert Burns's satire on the Calvinism of his day, see 'Holy Willie's Prayer', online at https://www.scottishpoetrylibrary.org.uk/ poem/holy-willies-prayer/ (21.1.24).

3 John Calvin, *The Epistle of Paul to the Romans*, Edinburgh: Oliver and Boyd, 1961 (first produced in 1540), 114. Cited in John Stott's commentary on Romans 5:12–21 in John R. W. Stott, *The Message of Romans*, Leicester: IVP, 1994, 160–2.

4 New Year's Eve.

5 It is entirely possible that Paul also literally wrote songs – the Christ hymn of Philippians 2:5–11 is often thought to have been written by the apostle.

6 Ricky Ross, *Walking Back Home*, London: Headline Publishing, 2022, 283.

7 Walter Brueggemann, *Finally Comes the Poet*, Minneapolis, MN: Fortress Press, 1989, 1.

8 At the time of writing, this is available on the BBC iPlayer; the episode referred to here is season 1, episode 6.

NOTES

Chapter 11: Community

1 Graham Reside, 'The State of Contemporary Mainline Protestantism', in James Hudnut-Beumler and Mark Silk, eds, *The Future of Mainline Protestantism in America*, New York: Columbia University Press, 2018, 53–4.

2 Dietrich Bonhoeffer, *Life Together*, London: SCM Press, 1954, 14.

3 Eric Metaxas, *Bonhoeffer*, Nashville, TN: Thomas Nelson, 2010, 527–8.

4 See Wayne Meeks, *The First Urban Christians*, New Haven: CT, Yale University Press, 1983, 77–80.

5 Tom Allan, *The Face of My Parish*, London: SCM Press, 1954, 32–7.

6 Alexander Forsyth, *Mission by the People*, Eugene, OR: Pickwick, 2017, 60–3.

Chapter 12: Scripture

1 Karen Armstrong, *The Bible – The Biography*, London: Atlantic Books, 2007, 162.

2 Cited in Armstrong, *The Bible – The Biography*, 162.

3 Cited in Armstrong, *The Bible – The Biography*, 163.

4 Cited in Alexander S. Jensen, *Theological Hermeneutics*, London: SCM Press, 2007, 70.

5 From the 2022 'Talking Jesus' report, available from https://talkingjesus.org/research (21.1.24).

6 Among mainline churchgoers in Scotland, only one in seven will read the Bible on a weekly basis. A study of mainline Churches in the United States found a slightly higher figure, about one in five (from David Bains, 'The Beliefs and Practices of Mainline Protestants', in James Hudnut-Beumler and Mark Silk, eds, *The Future of Mainline Protestantism in America*, New York: Columbia University Press, 2018, 74.

7 For an overview of Anabaptist scripture reading and its application to today, see Lloyd Pietersen, *Reading the Bible After Christendom*, Milton Keynes: Paternoster, 2011, 44–66.

8 Pietersen, *Reading the Bible*, 44.

9 It might be argued that many Free Churches have their primary origins within Calvinism and the Magisterial Reformation; however, their relative distance from civic establishment also suggests several characteristics more closely associated within the Radical Reformation.

10 The idea for which, many Scottish historians will be quick to point out, came from the Church of Scotland's General Assembly of 1601.

11 See Ian M. Fraser, *Reinventing Church* (self-published and undated) and also *Strange Fire*, Glasgow: Wild Goose Publications, 2004.

12 Published in Ernesto Cardenal, *The Gospel in Solentiname*, Maryknoll, NY: Orbis, 2007.

13 For a fuller discussion, see Armstrong, *The Bible – The Biography*, 197–201, and Jensen, *Theological Hermeneutics*, 84–7.

14 One notable attempt came from a revered fourth-century hymn-writer, referred to as Ephrem the Syrian, who put forward a number of possible explanations for the seemingly contradictory accounts that Judas had either hanged himself, or fallen in a field: it was possible, said Ephrem, that the rope had been cut after the initial hanging, thus leading to the fall. (See Matt. 27:3–10 and Acts 1:18–19 for the Biblical accounts.)

15 Irenaeus, *Adversus Haereses*, Book 1, Chapter 11, Section 8.

16 Augustine, *On Christian Doctrine*, Book III, 5, available at https://www.supersummary.com/on-christian-doctrine/book-3-summary/# (21.1.24).

17 Augustine, *The Literal Meaning of Genesis*, Book 1, Chapter 19, Section 39. By 'literal' Augustine meant something closer to our term 'authoritative'.

18 For a fuller discussion of Augustine, see Robert A. Ziegler, *Augustine of Hippo's Doctrine of Scripture: Christian Exegesis in Late Antiquity*, Primary Source, Volume C, Issue II, 2005, 33–9, available online. Augustine never went as far as to dismiss the historic accuracy of Biblical accounts; rather, he seemed to leave room for the possibility that in the fullness of God and time, all would eventually be resolved. Ziegler states that any attempt to match Augustine's understanding of historicity with later conceptions of inerrancy would be 'anachronistic'.

19 From Augustine, *On Christian Doctrine*, cited in Armstrong, *The Bible – The Biography*, 124.

20 The exception would be translations where the Church has long perceived an unjustifiable bias or those based on scholarly foundations which have been revisited in the light of later discoveries.

Chapter 13: Justice

1 Cited at https://www.thefreelibrary.com/His+minister+father+gave+him+a+sense+of+justice..the+fight+to+save...-a0165658056 (21.1.24).

2 Gustavo Gutiérrez, *Essential Writings*, London: SCM Press, 1996, 13.

3 See, for example, Gutiérrez, *Writings*, 104–8.

4 This report is hard to find on the websites of the churches which commissioned it. Typing 'The Lies We Tell Ourselves, UK Churches' into a search engine will produce a working link.

5 When delivering the 2017 McTaggart Lecture, available at https://www.youtube.com/watch?v=bOpMI3nWsrY (21.1.24).

6 Martin heard this remark through a translator and asks that it only be quoted with this important qualification.

7 I am aware of some recent debates which suggest Jesus was relatively 'middle class', but I am unconvinced. Mary's songs were the songs

of the poor; her and Joseph's sacrifice, at his birth, of a dove rather than a lamb is a significant clue (Luke 2:24) that they were from the poorest echelons of society.

8 Ernesto Cardenal, *The Gospel in Solentiname*, Maryknoll, NY: Orbis, 2007, xi.

9 Ian M. Fraser, *Reinventing Church*, self-published, undated.

10 See Walter Brueggemann, *Deep Memory, Exuberant Hope*, Minneapolis, MN: Fortress Press, 2000, 69–75.

Chapter 14: Land

1 Marjory A. MacLean, *Speaking from the Heart*, Edinburgh: Shoving Leopard, 2010, 32

2 Nan Shepherd, *The Living Mountain*, Edinburgh: Canongate Books, 2011, xxi.

3 In his introduction, Shepherd, *Living Mountain*, xv.

4 Shepherd, *Living Mountain*, xv.

5 Borrowing from David Wagoner's much loved poem 'Lost', published in the journal *Poetry* in 1971 and available online at https://www.poetryfoundation.org/poetrymagazine/browse?contentId=31968 (21.1.24).

6 John O'Donohue, *Anam Cara*, London: Bantam Books, 1997, 13.

7 This is a major theme of Tom Wright, *Surprised by Hope*, London: SPCK, 2007.

8 'The Holy Lands' was the name of our local neighbourhood.

9 Alastair McIntosh, *Poacher's Pilgrimage*, new edn, Edinburgh: Birlinn, 2023, 9–10.

10 See Jay Ruka's history of treaty breaking in Aotearoa, the role of missionaries (both positive and negative) and its implications for today in *Huia Come Home*, New Zealand: Oati, 2017. For a Native American perspective, see Richard Twiss, *Rescuing the Gospel from the Cowboys*, Downers Grove, IL: InterVarsity Press, 2015.

11 Ruka, *Huia Come Home*, 19.

12 Richard Holloway, *Leaving Alexandria*, Edinburgh: Canongate Books, 2012, 156–8, and also from subsequent conversation with John Harvey.

13 A copy of Lynn White's 1967 paper 'The Historical Roots of Our Ecological Crisis' can be found at https://www.cmu.ca/faculty/gmatties/lynnwhiterootsofcrisis.pdf (21.1.24).

14 Cited in John Stott, *New Issues Facing Christians Today*, London: Marshall Pickering, 1999, 136.

15 Richard Bauckham, *Bible and Ecology*, London: Darton, Longman and Todd, 2010, 37–66.

16 Cited in Bauckham, *Ecology*, 88.

17 Mary Oliver, *Devotions*, New York: Penguin, 2017, 347.

18 Originally transcribed in Alexander Carmichael's nineteenth-century *Carmina Gadelica* and quoted in Esther De Waal, *The Celtic Vision*, London: Darton, Longman and Todd, 1988, 8.

19 Here I am adapting a phrase of Andrew Rumsey in Andrew Rumsey, *Parish*, London: SCM Press, 2017, 181.

20 For an overview of parish as sacramental space, see Rumsey, *Parish*, 12. Rumsey also suggests that in a dislocated culture we miss parish in the same way that we miss God (p. 182). His use of the term 'Anglican localism' was behind the use of 'spiritual localism' used here.

21 Ricky Ross, *Walking Back Home*, London: Headline Publishing, 2022, 301.

Chapter 15: Song

1 The Swedish connection was through a remarkable activist and musician, Anders Nyberg. This importance of South African freedom songs is documented in the 2002 film *Amandla! A Revolution in Four-part Harmony*.

2 As spoken in the opening scenes of *Amandla!*

3 Quoted in Millar Patrick, *Four Centuries of Scottish Psalmody*, London: Oxford University Press, 1949, 4.

4 Patrick, *Scottish Psalmody*, 5; see also Finlay A. J. Macdonald, *From Reform to Renewal*, Edinburgh: Saint Andrew Press, 2017.

5 David Coplan, cited on Wikipedia, original article in French, Bennetta Jules-Rosette and David B. Coplan (2004). '"Nkosi Sikelel' iAfrika": From Independent Spirit to Political Mobilization', *Cahiers d'Études Africaines*, 44 (173/174), 2004, 343–67.

6 Cited from the seventeenth-century minister and historian David Calderwood in Patrick, *Scottish Psalmody*, 61.

7 The subtitle for *Amandla!*

8 Here I am borrowing the central image used by Lester Ruth and Lim Swee Hong in Lester Ruth and Lim Swee Hong, *A History of Contemporary Christian Worship*, Grand Rapids, MI: Baker Academic, 2021.

9 Patrick, *Scottish Psalmody*, 80–90.

10 This was the Westminster Assembly which also produced the Westminster Confession, which would become a key statement of faith for many Presbyterian denominations.

11 Patrick, *Scottish Psalmody*, 90–6.

12 Carol's organisation, 'Soul Marks', specialises in such an endeavour; see http://www.soulmarks.co.uk (21.1.24).

13 An insight which Peter credits to ecclesial architects Edwin Heathecote and Laura Moffatt.

14 John L. Bell, *The Singing Thing*, Glasgow: Wild Goose Publications, 2000, 56.

Chapter 16: Stillness

1 Surveys show that contemporary parents and carers spend considerably more time with their children, despite working longer hours; this is due to changing patterns of parenting which tend to allow children less time by themselves (see, for example, https://www.economist.com/graphic-detail/2017/11/27/parents-now-spend-twice-as-much-time-with-their-children-as-50-years-ago) (21.1.24).

2 From A. J. Swoboda, *Subversive Sabbath*, Grand Rapids, MI: Brazos Press, 2018, 57, and citing a survey by Karl Bailey in the *Journal of Psychology and Theology* (Fall 2005), 193.

3 Quoted in Nicola Slee, *Sabbath*, London: Darton, Longman and Todd, 2019.

4 Swoboda, *Subversive Sabbath*, 66.

5 *Vogue* journalist Anne Chamberlain, writing in 1969 and quoted in Swoboda, *Subversive Sabbath*, 66.

6 Quoted in https://www.huffingtonpost.co.uk/entry/seventh-day-adventists-life-expectancy_n_5638098 (21.1.24). Other reasons are a plant-based diet and strong social networks.

7 See Barbara Brown Taylor, *An Altar in the World*, Norwich: Canterbury Press, 2009, 130–1.

8 Swoboda, *Subversive Sabbath*, 57.

9 Henri Nouwen, *The Way of the Heart*, San Francisco, CA: HarperOne, 2016, 9.

10 For a good introduction to this prayer (and the use of the Russian *chotki* prayer rope), see Brian Heasley, *Be Still*, London: 24-7 Prayer, 2020, 26–8.

11 It is the practice of 'Centering Prayer' which has most sustained me, particularly as it is taught by Cynthia Bourgeault in, for example, her book *Centering Prayer and Inner Awakening*, Lanham, MD: Cowley Publications, 2004.

12 Bramdon. L. Whittington and Steven J. Scher, *Prayer and Subjective Well-being: An Examination of Six Different Types of Prayer*, Charleston, IL: Eastern Illinois University, 2010. The six types of prayer were adoration, confession, thanksgiving, petition, reception (i.e. contemplation) and obligatory prayers.

13 Quoted throughout Slee, *Sabbath*.

14 This is addressed by William Johnston in his chapter on crisis, in William Johnston, *Being in Love*, London: Fount Paperbacks, 1988, 82–9.

15 Walter Brueggemann, *Sabbath as Resistance*, Louisville, KY: Westminster John Knox Press, 2014.

16 Quoted throughout Slee, *Sabbath*; see especially her chapter 5: 'Then What is Afraid of Me Comes'.

Bibliography

Alison, James, *Faith Beyond Resentment*, London: Darton, Longman and Todd, 2001.

Allan, Tom, *The Face of My Parish*, London: SCM Press, 1954.

Armstrong, Karen, *The Bible – The Biography*, London: Atlantic Books, 2007.

Bauckham, Richard, *Bible and Ecology*, London: Darton, Longman and Todd, 2010.

Beeching, Vicky, *Undivided*, London: William Collins, 2018.

Bell, John L., *The Singing Thing*, Glasgow: Wild Goose Publications, 2000.

Bolsinger, Tod, *Canoeing the Mountains*, Downers Grove, IL: InterVarsity Press, 2015.

Bonhoeffer, Dietrich, *The Cost of Discipleship*, London: SCM Press, 2015 (first published in German, 1937).

Bonhoeffer, Dietrich, *Life Together*, London: SCM Press, 1954 (first published in German, 1939).

Bourgeault, Cynthia, *Centering Prayer and Inner Awakening*, Lanham, MD: Cowley Publications, 2004.

Brown Taylor, Barbara, *An Altar in the World*, Norwich: Canterbury Press, 2009.

Brown Taylor, Barbara, *The Preaching Life*, Norwich: Canterbury Press, 2013.

Brueggemann, Walter, *Finally Comes the Poet*, Minneapolis, MN: Fortress Press, 1989.

Brueggemann, Walter, *Deep Memory, Exuberant Hope*, Minneapolis, MN: Fortress Press, 2000.

Brueggemann, Walter, *Sabbath as Resistance*, Louisville, KY: Westminster John Knox Press, 2014.

Calvin, John, *The Epistle of Paul to the Romans*, Edinburgh: Oliver and Boyd, 1961 (first produced in 1540).

Cardenal, Ernesto, *The Gospel in Solentiname*, Maryknoll, NY: Orbis, 2007.

Carmichael, Alexander, *Carmina Gadelica: Hymns and Incantations*, Edinburgh: Floris, 1992 (first published in 1900).

Craig, Carol, *The Tears that Made the Clyde*, Glendareul: Argyll Publishing, 2010.

De Waal, Esther, *The Celtic Vision*, London: Darton, Longman and Todd, 1988.

Dillard, Annie, *Teaching a Stone to Talk*, New York: Harper Perennial, 1983.

Finley, James, *Merton's Palace of Nowhere*, Notre Dame, IN: Ave Maria Press, 1978.

Forsyth, Alexander, *Mission by the People*, Eugene, OR: Pickwick, 2017.

Fraser, Ian M., *Reinventing Church*, Self-published, undated.

Fraser, Ian M., *Strange Fire*, Glasgow: Wild Goose Publications, 2004.

Fraser, Liam J., *Mission in Contemporary Scotland*, Edinburgh: Saint Andrew Press, 2021.

Gagnon, Robert, *The Bible and Homosexual Practice*, Nashville, TN: Abingdon Press, 2002.

Gay, Doug, *Reforming the Kirk*, Edinburgh: Saint Andrew Press, 2017.

Gushee, David P., *Changing Our Mind*, 3rd edn, Canton, MI: Read the Spirit Books, 2017.

Guss, David M., *The 21 Escapes of Lt Alastair Cram*, London: Macmillan, 2018.

Gutiérrez, Gustavo, *Essential Writings*, London: SCM Press, 1996.

Heasley, Brian, *Be Still*, London: 24-7 Prayer, 2020.

Heelas, Paul and Woodhead, Linda, *The Spiritual Revolution*, Oxford: Blackwell Publishing, 2005.

Holland, Tom, *Dominion*, London: Abacus, 2020.

Holloway, Richard, *Leaving Alexandria*, Edinburgh: Canongate Books, 2012.

Hudnut-Beumler, James and Silk, Mark, eds, *The Future of Mainline Protestantism in America*, New York: Columbia University Press, 2018.

Jensen, Alexander S., *Theological Hermeneutics*, London: SCM Press, 2007.

Jenson, Robert W., *A Theology in Outline: Can These Bones Live?*, New York: Oxford University Press, 2016.

Johnston, William, *Being in Love*, London: Fount Paperbacks, 1988.

Kobes Du Mez, Kristin, *Jesus and John Wayne*, New York: Liveright, 2021.

Macdonald, Finlay, *From Reform to Renewal*, Edinburgh: Saint Andrew Press, 2017.

McIntosh, Alastair, *Poacher's Pilgrimage*, new edn, Edinburgh: Birlinn, 2023.

MacLean, Marjory A., *Speaking from the Heart*, Edinburgh: Shoving Leopard, 2010.

MacNeil, Tommy, *Sleeping Giant*, River Publishing, 2021.

Meeks, Wayne, *The First Urban Christians*, New Haven, CT: Yale University Press, 1983.

Metaxas, Eric, *Bonhoeffer*, Nashville, TN: Thomas Nelson, 2010.

Newell, John Philip, *Sacred Earth Sacred Soul*, London: William Collins, 2021.

Nouwen, Henri, *The Way of the Heart*, San Francisco, CA: HarperOne, 2016.

O'Donnell, Karen and Cross, Katie, eds, *Feminist Trauma Theologies*, London: SCM Press, 2020.

O'Donohue, John, *Anam Cara*, London: Bantam Books, 1997.

Ó Tuama, Pádraig, *Poetry Unbound*, Edinburgh: Canongate Books, 2022.

Oliver, Mary, *Devotions*, New York: Penguin, 2017.

Ortberg, John, *God Is Closer Than You Think*, Grand Rapids, MI: Zondervan, 2005.

Patrick, Millar, *Four Centuries of Scottish Psalmody*, London: Oxford University Press, 1949.

Pietersen, Lloyd, *Reading the Bible After Christendom*, Milton Keynes: Paternoster, 2011.

Reid, Harry, *Outside Verdict*, Edinburgh: Saint Andrew Press, 2002.

Rendle, Gil, *Quietly Courageous*, Lanham, MD: Rowman and Littlefield, 2019.

Root, Andrew and Bertrand, Blair, *When Church Stops Working*, Grand Rapids, MI: Brazos Press, 2023.

Ross, Ricky, *Walking Back Home*, London: Headline Publishing, 2022.

Ruka, Jay, *Huia Come Home*, New Zealand: Oati, 2017.

Rumsey, Andrew, *Parish*, London: SCM Press, 2017.

Ruth, Lester and Swee Hong, Lim, *A History of Contemporary Christian Worship*, Grand Rapids, MI: Baker Academic, 2021.

Shepherd, Nan, *The Living Mountain*, Edinburgh: Canongate Books, 2011 (first published in 1977).

Slee, Nicola, *Sabbath*, London: Darton, Longman and Todd, 2019.

Smith, Gordon T., *Institutional Intelligence*, Downers Grove, IL: InterVarsity Press, 2017.

Smith, James K. A., *Desiring the Kingdom*, Grand Rapids, MI: Baker Academic, 2009.

Smith, James K. A., *How (Not) To Be Secular*, Grand Rapids, MI: Eerdmans, 2014.

Stott, John R. W., *The Message of Romans*, Leicester: IVP, 1994.

Stott, John R. W., *New Issues Facing Christians Today*, London: Marshall Pickering, 1999.

Swoboda, A. J., *Subversive Sabbath*, Grand Rapids, MI: Brazos Press, 2018.

Taylor, Charles, *A Secular Age*, Cambridge: MA: Belknap Press, 2007.

Trueman, Carl R., *The Rise and Triumph of the Modern Self*, Wheaton, IL: Crossway, 2020.

Twiss, Richard, *Rescuing the Gospel from the Cowboys*, Downers Grove, IL: InterVarsity Press, 2015.

Whittington, Bramdon L. and Scher, Steven J., *Prayer and Subjective Well-being: An Examination of Six Different Types of Prayer*, Charleston, IL: Eastern Illinois University, 2010.

Williams, Rowan, *Being Disciples*, London: SPCK, 2016.

Wink, Walter, *Naming the Powers*, Philadelphia, PA: Fortress Press, 1984.

Wright, Tom, *Surprised by Hope*, London: SPCK, 2007.